THE POWER OF BELONGING

The Marketing Strategy
for Branding

SAID AGHIL BAAGHIL

iUniverse, Inc.
New York   Bloomington

The Power of Belonging
The Marketing Strategy for Branding

iUniverse books may be ordered through booksellers or by contacting:

iUniverse
1663 Liberty Drive
Bloomington, IN 47403
www.iuniverse.com
1-800-Authors (1-800-288-4677)

Because of the dynamic nature of the Internet, any Web addresses or links contained in this book may have changed since publication and may no longer be valid. The views expressed in this work are solely those of the author and do not necessarily reflect the views of the publisher, and the publisher hereby disclaims any responsibility for them.

ISBN: 978-1-4502-4576-0 (sc)
ISBN: 978-1-4502-4578-4 (dj)
ISBN: 978-1-4502-4577-7 (ebk)

Printed in the United States of America

iUniverse rev. date: 07/12/2010

I would like to dedicate this book to my dad, my mom and my son Rakan.

Contents

Brand essence: The brand essence is at the core of any brand life, brand positioning, and brand cultural ethos. These are the factors that build the overall look and feel of the brand. The processes of belonging, in this case, are the connective fabrics that allow these essences to be translated into multiple strategies, such as the specialty, the simplicity, and the adaptation. In order for a brand to find its way into the heart of an audience and induce that audience to become members of the brand, the brand must maintain its essence throughout the course of realizing the entire strategy by focusing on the basic principles of its strategies and message. For example if the strategy is to be different than the competitors, then the brand must uphold that for a long period, and the communication message must be consistent with the strategy. The essence is the heart of the whole process of moving the brand in clear directions.

Product: The product is not just about how good a quality the product is. It is about the essence of the product: its purpose and its functionality and then, as it becomes a brand, its activity. Many organizations that are very much product-oriented are too often out of touch with the consumer's needs and behaviors. Products must answer needs and purposes in order for them to reach the heart of the audience. If products are just about selling, then they have no real future in the marketplace. Making a product simply to make money is a waste of time and of money, because products designed and campaigns waged from such a paltry motive generally fail. A product that isn't marketed with a heart for the audience has no chance of finding its way into the audience's heart.

Perception: The overall look and feel of the brand from the point of view of the target audience, this is a concept derived from the necessity of human senses as they are moderated by a culture's taste and trends, and it affects each part of a marketing strategy, whether it be the name, the colors, the font when it comes to text, or the shape of the product or service. The perception is of fundamental importance to the overall life of the brand and to a proper understanding of how a marketing campaign and its product can make the difference as to whether the product goes nowhere, is a brief flash in the pan, is transformed into a lifestyle, or stands at the forefront of a game-changing trend. When you think of the major brands that you love or intend to buy, the primary factor that holds you is the perception of the brand that was created behind what constitutes the actual product. It was the perception that developed that initial contact, impelling you to explore the brand. And, as with designing the product and its campaign, the perception of the product is not up to the marketer—on the contrary, it is up to the marketer to have a feel for the perception of the people.

Brand identity: The identity refers to what industry you plan for your idea to enter, and even more specifically, what category of that industry. Identifying those parameters early on in a clear way can help you start building a market identity. Each industry and each category have identities and lives all their own. One must be different, but one must not try to reinvent the wheel, because the perceptions of each industry or category have been there for years. For example, look at Google or Yahoo; they are both in the Internet industry, but they each occupy the social media category. Look at McDonald's and Burger King; they are both in the food and beverage industry, but their brand identity is in the fast food category. Each identity has its own industry and category. Again, this is another thing that isn't up to you. You can't force your product into a category where it doesn't belong any more than you can convince your spouse that McDonald's might be a nice place to dine to celebrate your anniversary.

The brand positioning: Who could describe positioning better than Al Ries and Jack Trout? They are the creators of this revolution. Positioning is what you want your brand to be registered as and how your audience will remember you. For example, the brand positioning for Starbucks is "third place from home," meaning home, then office, then Starbucks. Facebook's positioning is connecting friends and family and people with whom you have lost contact. Volvo has long positioned its brand very clearly; they're the manufacturer you think of when you think about safety, because they have committed to and communicated their positioning better than any other car manufacturer. Also, the wizards behind all those companies and products developed a sense of those positions first as needs and desires of an audience that had yet to be met.

Brand culture: The brand culture is the world of associations and references you intend to create behind the brand, in order for your target audience to have an experience of your brand. Supplying your brand a culture is a means of creating a world for your brand that will support it and allow it to live and sustain its growth; the culture is what you will provide the audience in order for them to experience the brand through the ever-important vehicle of their human senses. A perfect example is the culture implied by the products and presentation of Ralph Lauren. He dominates the polo lifestyle of casual, sporty elegance and addresses it very well throughout the brand presentation—to such an extent that the brand is known more as Polo than as Ralph Lauren. Think of Timberland; the brand culture evolves through the outdoors, whether one is thinking of going camping or enjoying the forest and the mountain air or living in the winter beside a cove. The clear sense of culture that has been created behind those brands constitutes the overall conception among consumers that will assist the brand in pushing forward.

Brand experience: In order for the brand to make the audience feel the culture and allow them to live through the brand experience the experience is necessary as the audience's trail into the world of the brand. It could be comprised of visuals, images, or even the content that is in place around the brand communication. The experience is at the heart of how a brand culture is transformed into visual and other sensory content so that the audience can experience it. Have you ever picked up a Polo brochure? In it, you will be able to trace the culture experience throughout the all of the pictures and textual content. Have you ever picked up a Timberland brochure? It will take you through its brand experience from start to finish, top to bottom. The culture is created in order to be experienced.

Brand simplicity: The simpler the brand the better it can be understood, or on a more fundamental level, the better it can be experienced. The overcrowding of the brand, whether via an over-extended brand name and product lines or even through the brand owner's scattered communication, can leave the audience confused or, worse yet, leave them to fail to even form a perception of the brand. Simplicity helps you to maintain a focus and address the brand with one aligned message. Think of how simple and elegant Polo or Timberland is, and how focused. Starbucks is simple: it's coffee. Do you remember Kmart? Kmart tried to do and sell everything there was to sell, and when more categories that were focused came into the same industry, Kmart lost touch and its fate was clear. Wal-Mart has everything but managed to be clear in its brand positioning—namely, everyone knows that Wal-Mart undersells all its competitors, a mission to which it has always been committed. Wal-Mart is also close to nearly every neighborhood in America and thus has the reach to simplify its brand in that direction. The days are over when you can simply open a store, sell lots of nice things, and hope people will buy them.

Brand specialty: What happens when you create a product or service and you want to sell everything? You end up selling nothing. The saying may be old, but it's also true: the Jack of all trades is the master of none. Focus on your specialty; be the master of one thing. You can't be the master of millions. Starbucks specializes in upscale coffee and coffee drinks. If they sell other things, it's because those things, from mugs to music, go well with coffee. It's all about the coffee. Successful branders are able to let their audiences know they stand for something, rather than for many things, or for whatever they think they might be able to sell. Remember the number seven? That's a magic number in many cultures, perhaps because that's about how far our memory goes. For some reason we can relate to things in sevens. Seven wonders of the world, seven chakras, and seven heavens are some examples, among many others. How much diversity in your brand your audience can cope with isn't up to you; it's up to the audience's brains. Think in terms of the rule of seven with regard to your brand as being the outside limit of how far your family of products and messages can extend.

Brand adaptation: Once your audience adapts to your brand and the world you've created for it, the chain of growth is limitless, but only if you stay consistent and focused. Adaptation is the process by which the consumer comes to accept your created brand life, so that he or she can experience it in all its aspects. In order for adaptation to work, you must be clear in all your messages, keeping them well tailored and as simple as you can get them, so the audience can understand clearly what you are and what you stand for. The adaptation is the emotional link between the brand and audience.

Belonging: If all of the above steps are processed and aligned with all the five human senses, and the experiential part of the human personality those senses feed into, then the brand has a place to belong. Some might argue that I'm speaking about loyalty to a brand; well, yes, to certain extent. But belonging is more than that. It goes to the heart of appealing to all the audience's senses and their experience, while brand loyalty relies on marketing gimmicks used to gain audience loyalty, such as discount cards, frequent-buyer programs, and others. Belonging is about understanding a culture, not in a large-scale, abstract sense, but in a personal, experiential sense, and finding ways to appeal to people's most basic experiential selves, their sensory selves, in order to find ways to make your brand a part of their culture.

Chapter 1:

BRANDS START WITH AN IDEA

Introduction

Before I began to write this book, one word coursed through my mind a million times: *belonging*. One word can mean so much. Among its definitions, *belonging* means:

- To be proper, appropriate, or suitable: *A napkin belongs at every place setting.*
- To be in an appropriate situation or environment: *That plant belongs outdoors.*
- To be a member of a group, such as a family or club. *He belongs to my father's family.*
- To fit into a group naturally: *With my talent as a writer, I belonged in the writer's league.*

In the world of marketing, all these definitions come under the concept of branding. Everything belongs to something else in some sense, but brand belonging only happens if a brand is well conceived and then well nourished and maintained. It must live, just as humans need to avoid sickness and keep themselves in good health in order to continue to belong to life and not death. Brands, in fact, are much like humans in many respects. For a brand to connect with the right target audience, and thus to live, it needs to find where it belongs: the most *proper, appropriate, and suitable* segment of society for it. For a brand to belong to certain segment of society, it *must be situated appropriately.* To *naturally fit* its target audience, the brand's emotional attributes must become fused with the target audience's emotions.

There exists in the general public, and likely among many people who are trying to brand and sell products, a grave misconception, something of a conspiracy theory, really, about the power of the marketer. The argument goes that marketers sit in corner offices in beautiful buildings, arranging their piles of money and deciding what they want people to buy this year. Some people even suggest that marketers can even use this power to control people's brains. Nothing could be further from the truth. If you're one of the people who think that you could make people do anything you want or buy anything you want, if you only had enough money and could combine the features of your message in the right way, allow me to gently acquaint you with the truth: no message can catch hold unless the audience is already, in some sense, waiting for that message. No new product will find a market unless, on some level, people are already waiting for that product.

Successful marketers do have a power, but that power isn't one of manipulation and inducement. It's the power of being plugged into a culture, a position that starts with understanding and caring about a culture. It's also a power that's often based on a great deal of legwork. People who are designing next year's fashions aren't whipping up whatever pops into their brains and then making people like it. They are going out on the streets, finding where the hip kids are, the trendsetters, and taking lots of notes about what those hip kids are wearing. If you want to sell to a culture and have your brand become a part of its experience, you must know, understand, and like that culture. And get busy and keep up. Because in many parts of the world, particularly the parts that are interested in buying new products, culture is always on the move.

The Importance of Belonging

Belonging is therefore necessarily a strategy that begins in the initial phase of the idea, prior to that idea becoming a product. The idea belongs to the mind, and the mind visualizes the idea with an expectation of who the audience might be for that product, from both the demographic and physiographic standpoints, but more importantly, from a cultural standpoint.

Life is to belong. We belong to brands we love, and they to us. Throughout my nineteen years of experience in marketing, I have discovered that belonging is the most powerful word in marketing. For this reason, I undertook to write this book and address the belonging strategy, from start to finish. When a brand finds its way into the heart of the consumer, that's when it belongs. When brands belong to an owner or a corporation, they can then come to belong internally to the marketing department. From there, they can be developed in such a way that they can belong to consumers. The marketing department is responsible for infusing the brand with all the essence needed for the belonging strategy to work effectively.

We all belong to different brands. We follow brands, and we live the brands to which we belong. Most importantly, however, we admire and love our brands. To what brands do we belong? Only those that fulfill our needs and engage our human senses. You don't think you belong to a brand? You don't think you admire and love a brand? Consider this: some of the most fundamental aspects of most of our lives, whether products or not, frequently have many of the characteristics of brands. The parts of our lives we might not perceive as brands are simply those to which we belong the most: our schools; our churches, mosques, temples, or synagogues; our sports teams; our social clubs; our charitable organizations; our social movements (you honestly don't think "reduce, reuse, recycle" is a branding message?)—any entity that puts out a message, asks something of us, and creates in us a sense of participation and identification is a brand.

Cities, too. Cities are brands. Name your favorite city in the world and ask yourself: why is it your favorite? What is it about the city that comes into your mind? Is it a fact or statistic, or is it instead the cobbled streets? The noise and pace? The textures of the stones of old buildings? The lights of the city at night, as viewed from a walk in your favorite park? The smells and textures and sense of well-being you get when you visit your favorite restaurant? Your relationship with the city you love the most is based on your emotional experience. With all these things you love, you would have no idea of them it weren't for the way those things found their way to your being through your senses.

And those things that you perceive through your senses have found their way to a very fundamental part of you—a part that transcends thought, or skirts it entirely, and goes straight to your emotional centers, literally the base of your brain, the places where you feel, rather than simply acknowledging on an intellectual level pleasure and pain, light and dark, soft and hard, rough and plain.

The Importance of the Senses

The relationship between the senses and belonging is quite simple: the same parts of you, speaking in a literal sense, that register perception, those emotional centers that are touched directly by the apparatus of your senses, are the very same parts of you that feel a sense of belonging—that is to say, the parts of you that form attachments. Think of that certain smell that whips you immediately back in time to your grandmother's kitchen when you were a child. The feeling of belonging induced by that profound association, of something so simple as the sight, sounds, and above all the smells of a beloved woman baking, can be powerful enough to make a grown man weep.

When a company finds a way to make a brand belong, therefore, it is doing something powerful, purposeful, primal, and above all, relational. It is finding those centers of its audience's minds that have been formed of their sensory experience down through the years, finding the zones of positive feelings and pleasant relations and, in a state of respect for those feelings and associations, finding a place to live in that hallowed ground. That's a place where your product simply cannot take up residence unless it moves in through the window of the senses and unless you, whose responsibility it is to design and brand the product, have as much of a sense of and respect for the thoughts and perceptions of your prospective customers as you do for your own.

Why This Book?

In this book, based on my conviction as to the importance of this crucial junction between the senses and the feeling of belonging, I offer examples of how I personally have experienced some brands that have either *succeeded in belonging* or *failed to belong* to the audience for which they were intended. Some brands fail because the brand owner or corporation has intended the brand to work "on its own" and fails to consider the consumer's expectations. Some brands succeed because the brand owner or corporation strategically starts with an idea, defines its target audience, tests its product with that audience, positions its product to meet that audience's needs, and nurtures the product through innovation as the brand matures. These are the steps of belonging: taking an idea → to a product → to an audience → to positioning → to nurturing. I will cover each of these steps and their sub-steps in the book's remaining chapters.

I have written this book for people who want to change the way marketing is accomplished—and perhaps to a certain extent for people who are inclined to resist the idea of changing anything. This book will show you how invisible elements like the power of belonging can become the powerhouse of consumer loyalty. This book proceeds from the foundation and principles of the marketing mix and discusses brand profile, communication, and consistency over the course of brand innovation, even as generations change. In each section, I have described how a brand can belong to an audience and what steps need to be taken to ensure a brand belongs. These steps include considering such things as the emotional connection, the brand culture, the consumer's perceptions, and the brand environment experience. Also taken under consideration is the considerable extent to which a product's price as well is a belonging factor for a certain segment of the audience. The book also includes case examples from marketing departments and investors in the Middle East, including a discussion of the importance of having a regional marketing association that can undo the messes made by many industries in this region of the world.

A primary reason I have written about and used examples from the Middle East is that I come from the region. That is to say, I *belong* to that region, and for that reason I feel all the more keenly the ways in which this land I love labors under many misconceptions about the marketing process. However, I think this book will be interesting and useful not just for businesspeople from the Middle East, but for anyone who's interested in successfully branding a product, especially on a global scale. For such readers, it might be worth your while to think of the book's occasional focus on the Middle East as an opportunity to learn about how markets and businesses function for another market segment.

The culture of a brand includes the emotional processes required to develop the belonging strategy; these are the actual experiences in which the audience participates and which thus build the desired affection for the brand and infuse the brand with positive feelings. One of the strongest sources of impact with regard to a brand's potential to come to belong, as I have said, are the human senses, especially in terms of the potential customer's experiences with that brand. Brand owners that rely on these considerations are well on their way to building a growing population of followers and loyal foot soldiers for their product. If the brand owners are successful, not only will the brand belong, but the brand will travel to reach more audiences based on the enthusiasm of the first customers. The population belonging to the brand will thus grow—and the more the brand belongs, the more the brand performance engagement will grow along with its audience. It's a rare instance of a happy circle, in a world so full of vicious circles!

Sidebar: Who Owns Your Brand? You, or the Audience?

Claim! Who owns the claim to a brand? All too frequently, the answer to that question for a given brand is the expected one: the brand owners own the brand. But when owners claim the brand, they create a void in the process of belonging. Claim is all about the brand owner's ego. Rather than the brand being an icon that moves through the intangible but very real world of the consumer's perceptions and the consumer's set of claims, the brand stays tied up in the owner's ego.

But guess what? Selfish people aren't good at selling things. When it is simply the company itself that claims that its brand is the best or is of the highest quality, and they communicate this through all kinds of media, the brand really belongs to them as owners and not to the target audience. When a brand belongs to the owner and not the audience, that selfish sense of proprietorship leads to the brand's decline—brand loneliness, if you will, instead of brand belonging.

Instead, the claims should flow from the audience, with the owners creating an environment and culture behind the product that allows it to belong to its audience. For example, let's say you have created a retail brand of tea. You want your target audience to experience a certain culture you have created surrounding that brand, so you create a tag line of "My Day, My Tea." Suddenly, you've made that tea *belong*, though its culture, to the audience. The culture is the perception you create for consumers. Once they experience your tea, consumers can claim *publicly* that the tea brand is what it is.

The world of marketing changes throughout the years and the decades. We must keep in mind that change is good for the Middle East region; only through change can we forcefully compete with our brands worldwide. Unfortunately, we are living in a world in which the hype far outpaces the reality of doing what it takes to be good brand producers. We fear the challenge of our brands competing with the brands that are players in the global market due to our lack of self-confidence, or perhaps doubt as to whether the brand might be able to belong elsewhere, or perhaps because we've simply kept our aims too low. As a corporation or brand owner in the Middle East, you must ask for help and build a proper team to ensure that your process of brand building will be able to promote and sustain growth. Your personal satisfaction—and your commitment to what you want to do and how you want to do it—must be kept to the side: focusing on you and what you want is the beginning of failure!

Brand Belonging

Everything belongs to something, and something belongs to everything! It is the same with brands. Every brand has its own culture and community, much the same way a child belongs to his parents; we stem from the family tree; and we all belong to mother earth. From a starting point to an ending point—and every point in between—everything has a process of belonging. For example, you belong to your family. You belong to a certain religious denomination. You belong to a nation. You belong to an ethnic group. The list goes on. Belonging is an endless process that has great impact based on emotional attributes and the emotional connectivity of desire and wanting. Brands are no different from humans. They belong to a certain audience, and if built and nurtured correctly, they will live in the lives of that audience.

The science of how brands belong in our lives differs from other processes of belonging that are generated naturally, such as being born into a family. Brands are created purposefully and must be well identified from the initial process of an idea to the brand's name, the colors to be associated with it, and the entire brand profile. Not every idea can belong, however. An idea is still just an idea if it is not developed functionally to become a product and then developed into a brand.

When you generate an idea, it needs to belong to a particular audience. You then segment that audience so that the idea becomes more focused. Thereafter, the brand can develop into a product and eventually into a brand profile that takes into account the brand's union with the audience. A brand that belongs must be relational, which is to say it will live in dialogue with its target audience, changing and growing with them, or it will die. First, however, it must be designed, produced, and branded relationally as well. You can't expect to convince an audience to buy something when you haven't cared enough to check whether they need or want it.

The art of belonging evolves through many factors. For branding, these factors are consumer-oriented and serve as a way to create buying behavior. Essentially, belonging is a way for a brand to live longer. We have witnessed many brands decline in their first or second year because the owner planned nothing—from the idea to the market penetration. The costs of such a mistake are horrendous. Sometimes, companies fold or owners file bankruptcy.

This leads me to a very important idea: brands fail because brand owners listen only to their own voices and neglect to appreciate experts who can extend their knowledge and experience to assist them. (See the "Who Owns Your Brand? You or Your Audience?" sidebar.) Business owners often run to a safety zone by developing a "me-too" brand—essentially, they copy another brand in the market that is already successful, believing that in so doing they will be able to wiggle and advertise their way into a certain percentage of market share. The fact is that a "me-too" brand fails to belong anywhere. When a company enters the market with a "me-too" brand, it merely intends to replicate the success story of the already well-established brand. These tend to fail, however, unless they manage to find a way to *differentiate* themselves. Usually a company advancing a "me-too" brand enters the market thinking that pricing the product differently alone will beat the completion. Such a strategy can work for only few years; it cannot sustain a brand's growth and success.

A product can never compete on price alone. Instead, the strategy for the product's promotion should encompass the total brand life, from Identity, Positioning, Interaction, and thence to Nurturing so that the brand can come to belong in the hearts and lives of the audience.

As humans, we are nurtured by our parents and the earth, and so we come to belong to life. If owners fail to properly nourish their brands, then they will collapse just as humans would who go without sustenance. One simple, natural principle is that brands are born to live, and they will die without nurturing and maintenance. The primary nutrient for a brand is constant innovation, a vital process that will activate the living purpose of brands. While life belongs to us, so too does death belong to us. While each nation belongs to its continent and each city to a nation, so too do brands belong to the market and to an audience of end users. We all belong, and we belong to each other or the world at large in different ways. Ideas are created to become products, and products are created to belong to brands. The brand then belongs to the audience.

Chapter 2:

THE STRATEGY'S FOUNDATION: THE IDEA AND YOUR AUDIENCE

The foundations of marketing processes—product, price, distribution, and communications—are the points at which any marketing strategy begins to work properly. These are the foundations that create a sense of belonging between the brand and consumer. For the expected union to work, the development process begins when you begin to develop the idea into a product. When you develop an idea into a product, you must consider your target audience. So how do you decide who your target audience actually is? What trends are you seeing or hearing about regarding your intended audience? And what are the details about that audience, from demographics to psychographics? Let's look more deeply at your audience.

The Audience

A proper analysis of the target audience should set the idea's direction and determine how it should it be developed into a product. You should have the basic understanding that whatever product or service you develop, it needs to be designed specifically for a certain set of consumers. You design the product to account for your audience's likes and dislikes, not your own personal preferences. Considering the target audience in the initial phase of developing the idea is crucial if you expect and hope to develop the expected union. Starting with the development phase of the idea, your organization should be well aware of which entity in the market segment it plans to try to attract. Furthermore, the organization should understand the demographic and psychographics characteristics of that target audience. Demographics are things such as gender (male or female or both?), age group (youngsters? young adults? mature adults? elders?), race and ethnicity (Middle Eastern only? European? North Americans? South Americans?), and income (low income? middle income? wealthy?). Psychographics are characteristics such as personalities, values, attitudes, interests, and lifestyles. Is your audience progressive or more traditional? Do they enjoy being active or being sedentary? What do they like and dislike?

Once you have answered all these questions and developed a "picture" of your target audience, the big question to answer is with what percent of its potential "belonging" audience does the brand have a chance to identify? A small percentage would be 20 percent. The union or the belonging phase between the brand and the audience is a gradual process of growth, however, and it would be unreasonable to expect it to achieve 100 percent impact from the beginning. The audience members for which a brand is intended will take their time in testing and assessing a new brand. They use this time to size up the product's adaptability to their own set of perceptions and feelings in a process that determines whether the brand survives to belong in the life of the audience. The connecting fabric here is whether the brand reflects the needs of the target audience and appeals to all the target audience members' senses.

For all the reasons we've discussed thus far, it's vitally important that when you develop an idea into a product, the brand should be provided a way to move from the organization's mind to the consumer's mind. The organization should think and act like a consumer as it is developing the brand so that it can build into the product all the expectations that the consumer holds concerning the product. Consumers do not come to brands easily, however. The company or the organization must make the utmost effort to build a product for a population in such a way that it will inspire an intention to follow the brand, the created trend, or the brand culture. For example, one of the most successful consumer attachments was with hip-hop music. This connection occurred not only because of the music itself, but because of how the culture of the music was exported to the world along with its inherent cultural identity as associated with young African-Americans. Consumers may be fully inclined to follow a trend, but that trend must be well thought out and able to be sensed. The association with the senses that the brand adopts will benefit the brand by helping it grow widely. When thinking of marketing, you have to consider all the steps you must take prior to undertaking any brand communications.

The brand-belonging strategy will never influence the brand to live abidingly in the hearts of your target audience unless all the steps of marketing principles and all strategies are well planned, processed, and executed. So, consider that these foundational steps are essential in the process of building up toward marketing your product so that it can achieve its maximum effect. An organization with a vision has the lungs, the staying power, and energy to be sustained and to survive. An organization that is easily winded has its fate sealed right from the start.

The Idea

An idea has many angles; that is, it can be endless. An idea could be a product idea, a strategy idea, a public relations idea, or a communications idea. All these sorts of ideas have to have the potential to belong to the target audience. Again, only the right idea will work and attain results, while the wrong idea could send the wrong signal to your audience, and your product could flop. There are many considerations concerning how to generate good ideas in the marketing world, and each stands alone with its own purpose in the quest to achieve and deliver the best end results. We will look at each thought and emphasize its impact in the processes of belonging. Here are some examples of how an idea works for each sector of marketing.

Products Are Ideas

The thing you want to sell can be a tangible product or service, but whatever it is at the end of the day, it's a product to sell. In order for the product to be transformed into something that inspires a sense of belonging, the product must be durable, which is to say, *emotionally* durable, and what it delivers should be a *reason* more than a *purpose*. When I say "reason," I mean that the product should attain a firsthand engagement with the target audience. Again, the genesis of your product has to be relational with respect to the audience. Your reason for marketing a product can't be because you want to make money, or cash in on a trend, or prove your worth as a businessman. These are paltry reasons to do business, and they will result in failure.

One valid thing to consider regarding the product as an idea is how vital is the product to the market? To what extent do people need it? The processes of *need* in the market give the initial product idea the ability to penetrate the audience. For example, if you created an energy drink, would it fulfill a need? As an alternative to a regular carbonated beverage drink, yes, if you had been the first to the market; your product would have created a category, and *based on need*, the process of belonging to the audience would have been generated. The energy drink trend is a good example of how you make money with a product, which is to say, how you come up with a good idea for a product and how you don't.

The story of energy drinks is the story of someone in a position to market a product having the sense to pay attention to people and to have enough interest in those people to create the union between the brand and the intended audience because they knew what people were thinking about something as simple as soft drinks. Red Bull, the Austrian brand, hit the world market in the early nineties; today the brand is the dominant brand in the energy drink category simply because the brand was the creator of the category and the first to produce such an innovative product.

Once upon a time in the USA, people, especially young people, suddenly found that carbonated soft drinks seemed a bit old-fashioned. These young people were more health-conscious than the generations that had preceded them and had already rejected fast food. They were now in a frame of mind to reject the drinks that customarily came with fast food, as well: carbonated soft drinks. So, based on carbonated drinks' reputation for not being good for you, and their out-of-style association with junk food, these young people started casting around for something else. But what was there? Bottles of juice? Come on, they weren't babies! Coffee? Come on, their moms and dads drank coffee! What was there for the anti-junk-food generation to drink? Bottled water, then, they guessed. Eh. Flavored water, then. Eh. Bottled iced tea? Maybe for Grandma (although some caffeine would be nice). It was a smart, plugged-in marketer who cared about his or her audience enough, and knew enough about them, to see this gap opening, and who, by acting quickly and intelligently and with planning and great marketing, got to reap the benefits of filling that need. The important thing to note here is that the marketing department for Red Bull and others did not create the need through their marketing. They sized up the need, tailored their message to their potential audience—which they already knew, obviously, very well—and thus became a brand to contend with.

How don't you make money from energy drinks? How are they not a good idea? Simple: be the fifteenth guy to supply that need instead of the first. Not brilliant, not relational, not really an idea—it's just selling an energy drink because that's what they're doing these days.

Here is another example from the service industry based on an actual example of a need to belong. Because I have been living in Saudi Arabia for the past five years, I have had a lot of opportunity to observe the market and its process. Upon my initial observations, I was surprised to discover that proper marketing applications were not being applied in the area, when any processes were being applied at all. Eventually, the demand and the need for marketing consultants began to appear when companies realized they needed help to develop their plans and strategies. Was that a need? Certainly! Did it have the potential to belong? Yes! You may position your service or brand all you like, but having your product idea belong to the target audience should be your core objective.

Strategies Are Ideas

The core objective of any strategy in all aspects of marketing is to create a process whereby the idea may penetrate to the intended audience. In this case, what is a strategy? The initial importance of the strategy lies in its potential of being a way to reach our final goal. I have found as a consultant that one of the hardest things to do is to sell a strategy. This is because if your intended audience as a consultant does not understand the importance of strategy and its impact, then you have no service to offer. The client must understand the need for strategy. The communication of strategy consists of both visual and written content so that the prospective client can imagine the idea. This is the only way to deliver the idea of strategy at its initial phase. Once the concept is translated into actual, tangible action and is carried through so as to have its end result on the total performance of the company, then the strategy belongs to the audience and the company and is able to be appreciated by the board members. Effective strategies are workable strategies that instigate a process whereby they have the potential to belong somewhere in the heart of the company. A wrong strategy, on the other hand, can only hope to belong to the dark side of a company's history. Belonging means doing the right thing, and great strategies belong to great icons. For example, the strategy of brand positioning belongs to reputable marketing strategists Al Ries and Jack Trout. Their positioning strategy belongs to them and is now associated with their names for life.

The world of strategic thinking is behind every successful model of a business product and brand. Is brand more important than business? The marketing arm of the manufacturing industry is the service industry. Brands do count; strategic thinking and models do count. For local brands to reach a global platform, strategic thinking is obligatory. The Asian model is substantial proof these days of how manufacturing is bound up with the service industry. Consumer-produced products and fast-moving consumer goods (FMCGs) need all the science of marketing, not simply a logo.

Before all the clash of brand building and perception, you must get your hands on all kinds of proper product models and strategies on all fronts, such as corporate, marketing, and communication. All these should be aligned with your corporate vision. Today's counterattack of the commonly used terms ATL and BTL are strong advertising terms that ineffectual companies and deficient brands are using to attain results. For example, consider Boom Boom!, Code Red, and a few others in the Middle East's energy drink segment. Strategic thinking and processes are at the heart of a business and brand or of a brand and business. At the end of all the processes they are one. The point here is: why must companies ignore all the strategic processes of marketing and try to move so fast toward end results?

Today, companies in the Middle East try to activate their sales growth either by creating a broader reach or by using advertising. It is true that the wider you reach geographically the better chance you have for growth, but how about advertising? Does it help your company's sales to grow enough to justify the money you spend? Sales are forecast at the beginning of each year and in comparison to the previous year. My position here is this: companies too often intend to use advertising instead of strategy; they simply intend to over-communicate the same message over and over. The full force of growth can be modeled only through strategies, which is to say by innovatively creating model strategies that will attain a growth of 15 percent to 20 percent per year. The created model strategy should then be communicated by different platforms, such as through public relations and advertising—not just through advertising whenever the CEO or owner wishes, without having first drafted a strategy for growth! Business owners should consider measuring deliverables mid-term and long-term according to set timelines.

The art of the belonging strategy has a much greater impact when based on the laws of other successful strategies such as positioning. For example, once the brand is positioned in the mind of the prospect, the process needs to continue with a brand-belonging strategy and its associated principles. In such a case, the brand will live longer, just as it was intended.

Chapter 3:

PRODUCTS AND SERVICES THAT HAVE A CHANCE TO BELONG

What Exactly Are Products?

Even a service is potentially a tangible product. The next, very basic step is modeling the idea into a product, so that the product can deliver and supply the market need. But remember: products must first be ideas that have to be developed in order to belong to the marketplace. This development includes understanding that one must consider several elements prior to developing the product. Such consideration includes answering such questions as: What is the core idea and how could it be developed into a tangible product? What industry does this idea belong to? Which category of the industry does the product belong to? For example, if you are selling tea, is it to be sold in a tea shop that brews tea and sells it over the counter? You must draft your objectives clearly in order for you to come through on the deliverables, and these objectives must be strategically oriented in phases in order for you to be able to attain the goals you set. The point of drafting an objective is to see the expected deliverable that the idea or eventually the brand is hoped to achieve.

But First ...

I have observed what happens when organizations draft ideas without having clearly defined objectives, and the result has always been a blunder. The objectives, articulated perhaps in a few words or sentences, are the guidelines for the total process and the expected deliverable for the brand in order for it ultimately to be able to belong in the marketplace.

Once you come up with your product idea and figure out to which industry and category it belongs, then you must break that idea down so that it can be fine-tuned. In this way, you will find ways to make your product easier for your target audience to identify with. Next, you must ask yourself these questions: What is your best target audience, specifically? Where are they physically located, and what do they like? With which trends are they associated, or are you taking on the task of creating a new trend for them to belong to?

You must consider all these foundational stages prior to the product development phase. The process of modeling the idea into a product must take into consideration many external factors (such as those mentioned above) so that the product can be well geared for its external engagement. Think of the product as being like you when you were first born. The difference is that a product is born as an idea. We are all naturally born with a reason for our existence. Likewise, an idea is born in order to become a product or service that has a reason, a purpose it can serve through its existence. We all belong to our parents and to our family trees, which go back further than ourselves. So, we belong to something from years back and will continue the chain of belonging through our own children and grandchildren. We all belong to a brand name—the great entity that continues the chain of our family. In my case, I belong to the brand name Baaghil.

For the Duration

Likewise, products will always belong. Starting with the process of modeling the idea and going forward, the product should be consistent over the years as it is called upon to serve subsequent generations. The art of belonging as it relates to a product is to have the quality of eminence and its basic factors not be modified due to cost and other factors. Once the product is experienced, customers should have a consistent experience with the product each time thereafter. This consistency allows the consumer's passion for the product's belonging to be sustainable. Some big organizations consider cost cutting or changing a product's quality to a certain degree. The fact is that what you first started with must continue and not be modified in the midst of the actual product experience with the consumer. In this way, the actual product or the name of the product does not suffer a decline in the marketplace.

One of the vital issues a product may face is when the CEO or the head of finance orders cost cutting. These men are far from the realm of consumer belonging and should not have the ability to decide if the costs of producing the product should be cut by changing suppliers or sources to others that offer less quality and a lower price. And if they do have the power, they shouldn't use it! This is a grave decision to make, especially when someone from top management, who doesn't belong to or is distant from the market reality, is the one who makes the decision.

The actual experience should be in the hands of the marketing department and the firm's employees who are directly responsible for the consumer experience. If you are a consumer, I am sure you have experienced or come into contact with a product to which you built your sense of belonging based on you initial experience with it. Gradually the product sense changed, however, and you decided to move away from it.

As an aside, it seems important to note here that this idea doesn't work the other way around. That is to say, leaving a product alone is only of value when applied to not making the product cheaper or worse. Leaving a product alone is a mistake when it indicates a failure to improve the product in order to keep pace with the changing needs and desires of the market. A company and a brand that care about their audience or consumers—that is, successful companies and brands—must always strive to find ways to make the product line better, simply because the world changes and needs change. In other words, the sense of belonging has to be nurtured to be maintained. Just as the idea had to be formed based on a relationship with the audience, so the product has to be maintained and updated in relationship with the consumer.

Consider an example: the fact that you gave your spouse a lovely present for your first anniversary doesn't mean you're now set for life—no more gifts necessary! "I don't care about you? How can you say that, darling? I gave you flowers ten years ago, remember?" In marketing, you can't count on there being any such thing as a gift that keeps on giving, or an initial product conception and marketing strategy launch that you can expect to work in perpetuity. The relationship of the brand with the market must be maintained by the company, who must continue to think about the audience and its needs and desires and to do what it takes to have the brand keep pace with those needs or desires.

Otherwise, the sense of belonging, and consequently the brand, will eventually die, as some company who does care about the audience will step into the gap your inattention leaves.

The belonging factor begins from the idea and progresses until every part that is associated with the brand is completely aligned as one with the target audience. If you are considering this alignment, then you are a driving force behind a never-ending dynamic of product belonging.

Differentiation

The product content should also differentiate the product from its competitors, such that the product quality can stand alone among the typical human senses of smell, touch, taste, and other sensory experiences. Remember, the consumer's senses constitute the strongest driving forces of recognizing the product brand name, even above the actual advertising created to promote the brand. The product's differentiation factor can also generate a sense of belonging through the lightning-fast publicity of the simplest advertising method of all: word of mouth. That way of spreading word about your product is the most effective, because it is based on consumers' actual firsthand experience.

Word of Mouth

We've learned in recent years that customers are smart, and getting smarter. When they're watching an advertising campaign, they know that the people launching that campaign are trying to sell them something and that they are not necessarily looking out for the consumer's best interests in some philanthropic push to make sure consumers get what they need and are happy and content. Consumers know that advertisers are trying to sell them something. That is, the audience for the advertisement knows the difference between the internal motivation of the message— what the advertisement pretends to be about and what it says it's about, such as their desire to make sure your children get the best breakfast cereal possible—and the external motivation, which is obviously to make money. Looked at from that point of view, the company's choice to refer to your children's health can even start to seem a bit sinister from the point of view of the ever-more-cynical consumer. That is to say, they know the company is playing on their concerns about their children's health in order to palm off their sugary, starchy, bowl of nothing on unsuspecting parents.

In the Internet age, when consumers have far more resources from which to obtain information about a company's product than the company itself, you can expect the value of advertising to decline before it gets better. The information you provide to consumers in a thirty-second advertisement or on a billboard is paltry compared to information consumers can get on the Internet and review at their leisure. Plus, the information you communicate through advertisement bears the tinge of your external motivation, which in business is always to make some cash. Consumers' suspicion concerning advertisement, and their resistance to it, is something you can only expect to grow.

Such is not the case, however, for the most valuable source of information of all for consumers: other consumers. Advertising is nothing compared to word of mouth, both on the upside and the downside. If consumers have a good experience with your product such that they might be willing to buy it again, and such that they won't bad-mouth it if someone asks them about it, you've done okay that day as a producer of products. At least you've managed to start the ball rolling in the right direction. If consumers have a sufficiently good experience with your product that they're actually motivated to speak to their family, friends, and neighbors about your product, to actually recommend your product to them—well, that's simply the gold standard. No amount of money spent on advertisement can buy the powerful push that good word of mouth can bring to your product. Good word of mouth can even be so powerful as to make traditional advertisement pointless.

By the way, recent studies have found that hiring some celebrity to stand in for friends and neighbors, by way of hiring out good word of mouth, doesn't work anymore. The audience is well apprised of the external motivation of celebrities.

Word of mouth is powerful, and it's free. All you have to do is sell a good product. That's the good news. Are you ready for the bad news? Bad word of mouth is every bit as powerful as good word of mouth. If your customer has a bad experience with your product and you handle it sufficiently well that the customer isn't motivated to say anything, again, that's a pretty good day. You've broken even. On the other hand, if the customer has a sufficiently bad experience with your product that he or she is motivated to say something about it to his or her family, friends, and neighbors, that can be a dark day, indeed. Just as no amount of money can buy the sort of good will for your product that good word of mouth can bring, no amount of money can buy enough advertisement to dig you out of the hole into which bad word of mouth can put you.

To make matters worse from the point of view of business owners who are trying to unshelf shoddy merchandise, in the Internet age, consumers' means of spreading bad word of mouth are more efficient than ever before. There's no putting that genie back in the bottle!

Giving Your Product a Chance to Belong

In terms of cultivating belonging, you should treat your product as your service and your service as your product. Either way you have to exert maximum effort—not in lowering the cost, but in striving to make sure the product achieves the right sensory experience from the point of view of your audience. In the low-price category, those fast-moving consumer goods and products are identified through a marketer's creation of unique selling propositions. For nearly all the most common low-price category products, too many different brands are managed by several huge, reputable organizations. Most of these firms communicate to their target audience the heart of their unique selling propositions in order to differentiate their product lines from those of their competitors, in addition to all the claims they make in terms of their products being quality and premium.

For example, in the beverage industry consider once again the category of energy drinks. The geographical location is the Middle East, a market that I'm from and therefore with which I am most familiar in terms of product development and marketing. Over the past eleven years the market has witnessed an influx of imported brands of energy drinks, including the key players Red Bull and Power Horse. Red Bull, being the originator and creator of the category worldwide, established its presence as a viable product, and Power Horse, too, developed a following in the region. Each of these products had a different plan concerning target audience segmentation. When local beverage firms began to introduce their own energy drink products, price was the primary factor under consideration in the quest to have the product reach the heart of the mass market, and Saudi Arabia's Bison was the leader in this regard. Within a few years other local beverage producers introduced their own energy drinks, with eight new brands appearing out of the blue within just a few years after Bison had led the way, although Bison had already established a belonging process with its intended audience. The point is that, by mimicking Bison's pricing strategy, all the other energy drink products that came after Bison not only failed to create a unique product-selling advantage, they also cluttered the local energy category with nine brands, with more to come. These me-too products that are brands today failed to create their belonging process because they failed to identify their unique selling position, instead merely copying what had already been done.

One of the products for which I am a marketing strategy consultant is the energy drink Code Red, owned by a local Saudi firm. In order to create that total belonging process in the heart of the audience, the client was smart enough to elevate the level of energy on the drink as a product. As Code Red's consultant along with Local, a reputable ad agency, we decided to move in the direction of changing the color from the blue and silver commonly used among energy drinks to red. The colors not only differentiated the product, but helped push the product to become one of the top-selling energy drinks in the Kingdom. Mr. Hisham Al Easyi demonstrated his wisdom in taking steps to improve the channels of distribution in order to allow the product to reach the entire targeted audience.

Another example comes from the malt beverage category, in which a thousand players are competing, including multinationals. This category is not only cluttered by flavors, but firms have failed to identify a product-selling proposition. They all offer the same flavors and all push the same message, apparently not aware that only those products that came first to the local Saudi market, such as Musy and Barbican, can belong in the heart of the audience. The rest, in order to create their belonging process with respect to the audience, aside from the obvious matter of product differentiation, would need to address the actual experience that their brands would offer—that is, give their customers a real reason to care.

Services

The service industry, because it works primarily with intangible products, depends almost entirely on the force of human relations. How this sort of experience can be tangible and sustain itself as an actual product or brand is therefore an interesting question. Many in the service industry move away from the human experience and fall back on the claim, so commonplace as to be not worth saying, that their service is high quality.

First of all, service is a human thing. It's about relationships, and relationships don't happen without the engagement of the senses. Your five senses are key factors in not just acknowledging, but feeling the service that is provided. A good example comes from the airline industry. Airlines have many kinds of planes, but most of them have similar sorts of aircraft, so in this case audiences rely on the service and on their expectations of what they will perceive through their five senses. For example, airlines such as Singapore and Cathay rely not only on products they provide as great products, but additionally on the human relations they provide. My personal experience with Cathay Pacific was that the product they provided, and to top it all off, the human relations they infused with relational attributes, resulted in the brand not only leaving a lasting impression on me, but also making me look forward to flying with Cathay on my next business trip to the Asian Pacific via Hong Kong. The belonging process with regard to a product or service is to identify the differentiation factors and not to be redundant when undertaking to enter a war over market share.

Chapter 4:

THE AUDIENCE

There are plenty of people doing business out there who would like to skip considering what the audience wants. Believe it or not, there are people doing business who view their audience as their adversary, as if the whole thing were a game of football. In this view success is the ball, we're all trying to keep each other from getting the ball, I want to win, and that means you lose. From this point of view, your job as a businessperson isn't to satisfy the customer but to put one over on him. If you can stick it to the customer that day, that's when you've had a good day.

My message here is that business can be a win-win situation. Not only that, but balancing the needs of the consumer with the needs of the business is how things are going to be done in the future of business—and perhaps how they should have always been done. Now, however, that consumers have so much information at their fingertips, and now that so much of this information is so much better information than they used to have, businesses no longer have any choice but to consider their audience.

Previously, we've discussed the importance of considering your audience with regard to coming up with your product or idea. Here, we begin the process of learning how to extend this understanding of your audience to encompass the marketing phase of your enterprise.

Who Are the People in Your Audience? Where Do You Find Them? What about Research?

Finding a target audience from among a total population is not something you can accomplish in an instant. You must understand who your prospective audience members are and what their needs and behaviors are. From there, you can create and eventually grow your audience, from ten to one hundred and further, depending on how you manage your product and brand. Expecting your target audience to figure out the product life cycle by themselves while you sit in your office and assume they can do this on their own presents a problem for the growth of your brand. If that's your only strategy, you will probably witness your brand becoming stagnant and being reduced from the initial one hundred consumers to ten, shortly before you have to shut down your business.

The art of belonging with respect to the audience means understanding their needs and how you can maintain and manage those needs with respect to your product. It means being in a relationship with your customers. You must keep your brand at all times in line with your consumers' interests. Doing so is a way of having your brand grow with the audience as a result of the union of belonging. When you think of a target audience, think of the processes that will make them stay and belong to your new brand. Consider all the factors of your consumers' engagement with the product, starting with their behaviors, their senses, and the terms of their emotional belonging.

How Does an Audience Belong to a Brand?

For the audience to belong to a brand, the consumer's initial experience must be considered the most vital contact. When a consumer is trying out brands, he or she is in a testing phase, through which he or she explores the product's potential and discovers his or her likes and dislikes. This being the case, the terms of belonging are variable, and they depend on the product's performance with the consumer. With that important and risky first encounter in mind, the organization's managers should look to the product's consistency factor in order for the experience to earn the consumer's favor and for the product to leave a good impression.

The total experience of the consumer's encounter with the product is the brand's living form. It hinges on the consumers' expectations of the product's performance and deliverables—what can the product do for the consumer? The consumer's frame of mind is not to take things lightly and to just let little things go, especially when the product is a new, incoming brand. The brand must leave a completely positive impression on the target audience. Don't forget the discussion above concerning the importance of good word of mouth! The art of belonging here depends on the union between the brand and the consumer, which includes the initial phase of attachment based on the product's appeal to the five senses and the emotional connection created between the brand and the consumer. When mentioning emotions, I'm referring to the "love" attributes that represent the consumers' likes stemming from his or her first experience until that first experience has ended. This attachment, as may be obvious, is built around attachments and associations the consumer already has and what's missing from his experience—not from your perception, but from the consumer's.

It is essential for all of these factors to be carefully prepared in order for the consumer to employ his or her buying power and hopefully to spread the word about the potential of this brand. In the previous century, most companies by and large competed on such playing fields as price and brand benefits in their efforts to gain market share. Today, the world has changed. You must attract your audience by considering their minds and behavior patterns. You must consider the consumers' senses and emotions. These attributes have the strongest power over whether the quest to create brand belonging on the part of the audience and to maintain that position consistently will be successful.

Audience Relationships vs. Loyalty Programs

Some readers might jump in here and say that what I'm saying sounds like a call for a consumer loyalty program. There's an important distinction to be made here, and I don't believe it's just one of terminology. Consumer loyalty programs ask the consumer to be loyal to the brand based on the name itself even if nothing is offered to the consumer except simple benefits. If the company does not meet the consumer's basic human needs, and if the brand does not perform close to consumer expectations, then how do you expect the brand to belong? Exactly! Loyalty gimmicks are the sort of quick-fix program that may actually scare your audience away. They aren't a way to get to know consumers and find out what they want and need, what their world looks like, and how your product might fit into it. They're a lazy company's way of skirting that process! With loyalty programs, customers may feel that the brand is shoving itself in their faces and asking them to be part of something that they may not have experienced on an emotional level. They may also create a situation in which consumer's suspicions about your external motivations come into play. Are you really rewarding their loyalty as you say, or are you just trying to figure out a way to make them buy more of your stuff? Offering consumers a loyalty program before you've even gotten to know them is sort of like a new neighbor who invites you to go on vacation with him during the encounter when he first introduces himself to you. One's reaction is not "Wow! He must be a really special and generous person!" It's "Wow! What's wrong with that guy? What in the world is he up to?"

Unlike loyalty programs, product branding gets personal— starting with the content and the profile. Once the brand succeeds in becoming personal, you have begun to develop the art of belonging. In the case of a service, if personalization is not taken seriously in designing the contact between the audience and frontline staff, then the art of belonging will not be realized.

Let me give you an example. I travel constantly. I can name three great airlines that have left me with a lasting impression of being able to give the person-to-person, human touch. These brands are on a growth path. One of them is based out of Hong Kong, Cathay, which I've discussed above, while the other two are based out of Singapore and Dubai. All of these airlines have left me with a good impression, but just as importantly, each of these airlines has given me a distinctly *different* good impression. They have delivered different types of services and have provided me with different experiences. The service experience for the Dubai-based airline was its luxurious presentation of in-flight products that give one the perception of flying first class. The experience, which worked through all my senses, caused me to like this airline based on the product presented. The negative reactions I experienced with the airline had to do with the emotional connection. I felt that the service exhibited a lack of the sort of relational feeling that should compose the overall brand deliverable. On the other hand, the Hong Kong and Singapore airlines delivered products at the peak of my expectations concerning service, perceptions, and emotional attributes, to such an extent that I am always eager to be on their flights to any location, be they to the Far East or from the Far East back home. My reasons for this preference are that as consumer, I *lived* my expectations of the product and total service, from the initial contact on board to the in-flight products and personal attention. Both brands left the sort of impression, for instance, that drove me to mention them in my book. The brand perception delivered the total experience a consumer would expect from a major airline that is striving to compete on a global platform.

Segmentation

I have watched many categories of products in terms of their target audience expectations. Some are products that have audiences that can be classified according to income level, and that demographic consideration is how they built their brand so as to belong to a certain segment. There are many things to consider, however, in segmenting your target audience. As mentioned, many companies consider the price factor to be the key element in segmenting audiences. Others consider the brand value deliverables. Consumer segmentation means servicing different needs. There are products that are amenable to the use of very simple models. For instance, as with regard to gender-based segmentation, Tampax is for women, while condoms are for men. Diapers are for babies, while shaving cream and blades are for grownups. (Though it's the parents who buy diapers, and it's often women who buy shaving products as gifts for men, so even these seemingly simple things can get complicated quickly.) Larger segmentations can even be broken down from general organization groups into sub-groups. Usually successful brands stay focused on a specific segment, even if the brand attains 10 to 15 percent of its targeted audience. Once the segment is well focused, then the brand deliverable to this certain segment is clear, and the process of belonging can begin in earnest.

I have witnessed a strategy wherein the product tried to be a general brand to all consumers. The national airlines following this strategy, which are found mainly in Third World countries, have one process of belonging. The company simply has and operates under the expectation that citizens of the region it serves will belong to it and prefer to travel on it. At the same time, however, the company neglects all the processes associated with belonging, from product and service expectations to brand deliverables.

On the positive side, and by contrast, I have kept an eye on an African airline based out of east Africa that has positioned itself well with respect to the entire continent and has thus expanded its network to include almost every major African city. It pursues a sense of belonging with respect to the continent based on its clear positioning and tagline—"The Spirit of Africa." This airline, with its successful track history, has competed with global airlines by focusing on its target audience and by properly segmenting the continent of Africa as its directly targeted audience for all their outbound and inbound air travel. The airline's strategy is to expand throughout the continent under a sense of belonging to the continent as the airline of Africa. The airline never intended to focus on pricing strategy as a form of belonging, even though it operates from a continent in which personal incomes are among the lowest in the world. Instead, they have positioned their brand to send a clear signal to their target audience in terms of ethnic and cultural belonging.

Meeting Audience Expectations

Audiences have expectations, and many firms fail to deliver on those expectations but instead simply try to shove their brands down their audience's throats. That's no way to gain the maximum advantage. It is the beginning of failure. Organizations that produce brands are a bit inclined to be arrogant and distant from the consumers' needs and to resist innovation. They labor under the belief that audiences will accept their products no matter what as long as they have the will to sell. That is a false thought and a failing assumption that will lead a brand to falter from its initial engagement. Looking at that situation, and knowing such companies intimately, I have frequently sat and thought to myself, if companies intend to produce products or services, what is it that keeps them from clearly determining and investing in their audience by understanding their needs and the specifics of their audience's behavior? What keeps companies from realizing the need for audience differentiation and for providing something that can fill a need?

The perfect example for me is Internet search engines. Early on, Yahoo was always the best-known search engine. It was the first major player; it is still a strong competitor among search engines and has been throughout its fifteen-year lifespan. Then along came Google, who differentiated its process by setting out a new vision and experience of what it means to search on the Net.

Google had a strategy of innovation, innovation, innovation, all to make things better for searchers. It added lots of whistles and bells to the search engine, but none that got in the way or served as a distraction. All were meant to make the search easier and better. It provided spell-check and gave options to its audience members who may not have typed search terms correctly. It continued to refine its algorithms for anticipating what searchers were looking for and providing results in an ever more simple-to-consume format. Its sheer superiority, captured through a commitment to its target audience and its willingness to innovate, became more and more evident until it captured the leadership in the market.

Google didn't stop there, however, but continued to provide services that enhanced users' experiences. Google's management is among the most flexible in the history of large companies. Its leadership has a policy of letting the brilliant programmers it hires try things and put them up, instead of deciding from the top down what people need and whipping its workers in line to produce it. And if the things those workers try work out, always with respect to what the audience needs and wants, then the company makes sure those innovations find their way to the customer's fingertips at lightning speed. The brand's adaptability itself has become part of its brand perception, until today Google is known as the giant among Internet search engines.

Then as if that weren't enough (one senses that it's never enough for this company) Google introduced Gmail, an innovative e-mail system that had many user-friendly options. It managed to capture much of the Yahoo mail and Hotmail audience. I have a friend who's a big Gmail user, and he shared with me that it's almost with nostalgia that he remembers the pre-Gmail days of struggling with proprietary e-mail programs on his computer, or Internet-based services with all their limitations and expense. He remembers fantasizing about finding an Internet-based e-mail service that could do all the things Microsoft Outlook could do but wondering how much a service like that would cost, and then Gmail showed up, almost as if Google knew what he was thinking. Of course, they did know, because they made it their business to know. And as for cost? It was free! Once again, Google's leadership and spirit of innovation won the day for its e-mail service as it had done for search engines. I also think that Google was smart in the choosing of the name for the e-mail service, Gmail, which used only the first letter of the already well-known brand name based on its success in the search engine business.

Today Google has progressed to such an extent that the Google team has moved its brand into many services that a user can take advantage of by signing in to his or her Google account, but I would simply state that I believe Google has made a mistake in doing so with the proliferation of such brand extensions as Google Reader, Google Wave, Google Earth, Google Maps, and so on. Their most famous misstep in this regard recently was with the rollout of Google Buzz, an entry into the social networking market. I believe the most innovative products will always be remembered as Google products but not, for instance, in the case of their web browser, Google Chrome, given that there were so many others that had come first, such as Internet Explorer, Netscape, Firefox, and Safari, and the list goes on. I thought Google had a clear strategy in brand naming: to clearly incorporate or directly use the Google brand name on their most innovative search product categories, and for other, less-innovative offerings, to give them a different name, as was the case with their mail system, which they called Gmail. Today the Google name can create confusion in the audience based on the presence of so many Google product names, when all the audience can really remember is the search engine and the Google Earth portions of the search market. The high-tech savvy among us aside, I think the general public that uses the Net for all sorts of different services will not be interested in all this brand extension, given the fact that the mind can remember up to seven things at a time with regard to one name and that only the first few they experience are able to take up permanent residence in their minds.

Chapter 5:

BELONGING AND THE STRATEGIES OF PRICE, REACH, AND POSITIONING

Price

The strategy of selling low and thus gaining more customers has prolonged the lives of many businesses. Some organizations compete from the position that they will always sell low to win the market, rather than basing their products on brand credentials and positioning. How long can such an organization sustain growth with more brands always coming into the market? The factor of price categories is a valid one from which to sustain growth, taken in the context of all the other elements that we have discussed and the ones we will subsequently discuss, all of which should live in total synergy.

A good example of a successful price strategy resulting in belonging is the case in recent years of Sharjah, the third largest of the UAE-based airlines. Sharjah introduced a low-price airfare strategy in contrast with the major US-based airlines. The airline captured inbound and outbound flights in the Middle East region, moving into second place in the category after Kuwait Airlines, which has a long history. The Emirates-based airline achieved a belonging status by means of a good product-modeling description, a price based on the target audience, proper brand building, great positioning, and well-executed marketing outreach logistics through the Internet. Another element worth considering is that, in comparison to Dubai Airlines, Sharjah is well positioned to be the region's premier low-price carrier, while Dubai is positioned as the region's premier high-price carrier. Most lower-income expats live in Sharjah and commute to Dubai for work. This example serves to illustrate how the price factor can play its part among the many factors of belonging. It could support a category, and that category could come to belong to a city or a nation as part of an ongoing dynamic that can serve to sell the whole entity in its brand processes.

Pricing can do more than that, however. It may help a company hold a category for a brand or help to differentiate a product in the branding process itself. For example, the Kuwait-based low-price airline was the first to introduce the low fare. It failed to stay competitive, however, even though it was first, because it did not position its product in the public perception as that of a low-priced airline, and so it never came to belong in that category. It never communicated the purpose of providing lower airfares or took steps to build up the brand in such a way as to send the actual low-price message. The short of it is that the airline never communicated its brand positioning in such a way as to position it to belong somewhere, and so the belonging never occurred.

The simplest processes of marketing are distribution and price. These are the things that every company must take into account and take action on. Companies doing business in the modern world enter into an endless price war at full force, with market reach being the main goal of their strategy. But things have changed! Every industry is cluttered with a variety of categories, and each of the categories often contains more than ten brands. You must create positioning, therefore, to advance the brand into the belonging phase. Only by taking steps to achieve that position can a brand hope to sustain its growth.

In the case of low-price positioning, in order to work, this strategy needs additional marketing processes to keep it company, such as keeping the brand consistent so that it comes to stand for low-price positioning in all its aspects. That part of the strategy requires good internal brand communication so that the brand can be matched well to the audiences' needs.

Audience need is a major factor of belonging that intersects with a pricing strategy. For instance, if we think of a shampoo that costs $2, clearly the company that makes that shampoo wants to position the brand as affordable to the masses. The question is, though, what if that is the only branding process designed to make the shampoo belong to the audience? For the brand to survive, it can't be the only tactic. The company needs to further act to communicate the brand, emphasizing the price by the use of strong visuals that will serve as a way toward belonging in the heart of the audience. Also, the company should consider other factors, such as the brand culture, which must be built around the lifestyle of the audience, including, certainly, repeating the price in all related communications.

Price is often a strong consideration in the fight for a company to stay competitive, but a good pricing strategy alone does not always do the trick. If you're missing the art of positioning and belonging, a pricing strategy cannot be effective. You're dealing with humans and their needs. Because you are working with humans in terms of brand communications, you must consider that the heart of the process is to meet their needs. And this is done in part by implementing the processes of positioning or brand belonging. This process becomes more effective when it appeals to the audience's five senses. By taking that road to the most fundamental part of the audience's thinking, you can drive home a convincing argument through the vehicle of both the minds and emotions of the audience that they *need your product*.

Usually, big organizations use the price factor from the marketing mix as their core means of delivering their organizational goals. In addition, organizations tend to believe that the price factor or promotional approaches to sales are the ultimate means of bringing new consumers to the brand. While this may be true to a certain extent, price is only one of the elements of the total process that allows your brand to work for and belong to consumers. Is price a strategy? Yes, it is, but other strategies tend to work better. Examples of such strategies are finding a category that is open to the domination of competitors and being the first in a brand category. Would pricing work if you were the second or the third brand in a category? I doubt it, because then the strategy would defeat the purpose of being the first and only product in the category. Remember the "me-too" or Me2, brands, those look-alike products? In such a case, the profit margin would be riding a thin line, and the organization would have to do business at a great volume and maintain that volume in order to survive.

If such were the case, however, an organization pursuing this high-volume/low-pricing strategy must keep its eyes on both the sides of the coin at once. For one thing, the supplier must reduce its selling price such that consumer movement to the brand is based on volume sales. Only in this way can the organization achieve its goal. That sort of business model can be very risky, especially when the product is not first in the category. If the volume sales required for survival do not come through, or another company finds a way to play the high-volume/low-pricing strategy better, then the organization's thin line of profit is gone, and the company will be operating at a loss.

The important idea here is that the selling price to consumers is not the prime factor in the belonging strategy. Instead, creating the proper brand build-up and establishing the product as an idea in a way that embraces the consumers' needs are vital considerations for any company in order for it to attain volume sales.

All too often, however, organizations focus only on consumers buying price and suppliers' selling price. Factors in the middle regarding building a brand model to achieve the organization's ultimate goal are all too often neglected. When using a pricing model that implies a thin profit margin and a model in which the brand is designed and built so as to belong to the consumer, the price has to be consistent. In that event, the reduction in cost should come from the supplier, and the ability to reduce those costs to the firm may depend on how the firm plans to increase its sales volume to pressure the supplier to make future cost reductions.

Pricing is, indeed, a major factor, especially when you have a brand that is targeting lower-income groups. The belonging process in this case is not the total brand build-up nor the brand itself, but the product and the price together. Price in this case reflects the consumer's mind and what the consumer will consider. When your strategy relates to pricing, the emotions and brand perceptions are not constant factors. Regardless, the brand build-up and the communication must be in place in order for you to be able to reach consumers with your message. So, for the price factor to be strategically correct, it must be communicated on every piece of information associated with the brand name so that the low-price brand message is communicated clearly.

Overall, price is a sensitive issue when dealing with target audiences, but you must consider many other factors for the product to be properly delivered and to have the product find its way to appropriate destinations, such as retailers' outlets. What is a product with "market reach," or more commonly, "distribution"? Distribution is another fundamental of marketing. If an organization does not concentrate its efforts on mass distribution based on a mass-branded product, this failure can hurt both profit margins and product reach. Having your mass-marketed brand everywhere makes your product more accessible and creates the potential for better sales. If consumers know your product, but it has less reach, then you have declining options in terms of marketing strategies, brand communication strategies, and tactical strategies.

Reach

Market reach or distribution is another basic principle of marketing. Without product reach or distribution, your company has nothing to offer consumers, even if it has a great product, because it has no means of reaching those consumers with that product. Your product has to be distributed in such a way that communications will be able to reach your target audience and subsequently in such a way that your target audience can purchase your product. Your geographical reach needs to reach the widest audience appropriate to the segment of the market you are targeting. You should avoid distribution to areas where your product will not belong to the audience—where no one in those areas will purchase it. I often hear claims that a brand is not selling because the owner has underestimated brand distribution. For example, a low-priced brand positioned in high-end supermarkets and in high-income suburbs of a city will not sell. The owner positions the product in this way for mysterious purposes perhaps having something to do with self-satisfaction, but this sort of approach does not elevate the brand. In fact, such a strategy serves only to kill the belonging processes of the brand. This is true even if the owner estimates he can attain a 15 percent share of the market by being in high-end markets. Consider a different case. You have communicated your brand to a certain audience, and that audience is where your brand belongs. Where do your target customers shop? Where can they purchase your product? If you start thinking about distribution starting with the initial process of the idea and brand positioning, you will know where your brand should belong.

Extending Reach and the Problem of Internet Commerce in the Middle East

In this book, I do not spend a significant amount of time talking about reach and its associated channels of distribution. It's a simple market reality. The one point I want to get across about it is that you must align your distribution channels through the process of belonging once the brand is positioned. In today's market, there are many ways to achieve reach beyond physical market reach. The Internet, for example, has opened up my region to pursuing a global reach. The Internet, then, is one of the channels that most companies in the Middle East should consider in their efforts to communicate their brands to their target audiences.

In the Middle East, however, we have a problem with the Internet, and that is penetration. Middle Eastern audiences tend to trust American and European sites in terms of conducting online transactions, but tend not to trust transactions conducted on local sites. And, while they trust the online use of credit cards with respect to government-owned establishments, they tend not to trust such transactions with respect to the private sector. Thus, this channel of reach can be improved only if the private sector takes the initiative to build consumer confidence in the Internet both as a vehicle for commerce and as a product.

We also have to consider growth over the previous five years. Demographically, it is the new generation that is the growing consumer segment with regard to online purchasing. They are, indeed, your future prospects, and speaking of belonging, there is no question that they are a generation that belongs to the World Wide Web. Factors surrounding online purchasing should come to be seen as being among the primary responsibilities of every organization, and the ministers of trade in the Middle East should work to raise an awareness of a business model that incorporates that responsibility. In this way, online purchasing will come to belong in the future of trade. Come to think of it, this vacuum in terms of service—this ongoing need—might represent a good business opportunity for someone who can find a way to make credit card transactions on the Internet trustworthy from the point of view of Middle Eastern consumers and merchants.

The possibility of such an entrepreneurial rescue aside, consumer confidence can only be attained once organizations take steps to provide secure consumer trade transactions via online verified systems much like the ones that most Western brands use. As long as such factors are not in place, then the belonging process of the consumer to the channel of online buying will be void. If the organization itself is not confident of online buying processes, why would it expect its target audience to trust that channel? Trust must extend from the top to the bottom in order for it to be effective. Trust must be afforded to everyone in the organization, and thence to the customers, so that the potential magnitude of the channel to extend a company's reach both domestically and globally can be realized. The simple truth is this: for online buying to occur and belong to the growing process of this avenue of commerce, government ministers and organizations alike have to establish laws that will secure enough consumer confidence that consumers will be encouraged to interact with online buying and treat online shopping avenues as trusted destinations.

We have seen government entities introduce online bill payment options over the past few years, but organizations have fallen behind in even starting to build confidence in the Internet as an avenue of commerce. On the other hand, banks in the Middle East are leading a significant initiative to develop the logistics of providing online buying processes. The undertaking might be a slow process, but this development of the channel nonetheless seems promising. The audience that belongs to online buying is the current generation, which constitutes the majority and is still growing every day in the Middle East. This younger generation trusts online buying with regard to US-based brands, but has never been given the opportunity to experience such a relationship with domestic brands. Perhaps it goes without saying that the failure of Middle Eastern businesses to develop the potential of this relationship constitutes the loss of a source of potential revenue.

When a consumer in the Middle East buys online from a domestic online site, he should be able to trust that he can make the purchase with his locally issued credit card. In this way, the consumer can personally monitor the transaction until the product is delivered. Once this experience is able to take place and the online buying habit continues, the consumer will share his or her positive experience with friends, family, and co-workers. Following upon such a word-of-mouth process, online buying will begin to belong to a growing audience.

The initial contact of the potential customer on this channel as a means of consumer activity and product delivery is the place where the trust is forged or broken. For the channel to work, however, local Middle Eastern brands should be consistent. Some are consistent for a few months, but then the process of belonging to the audience drops, and the companies experience a high number of complaints regarding delivery or other issues. In addition, the shareholders and business owners of many corporations too often have a tendency to constantly manage change that affects the entire process of deliverables for the consumer.

Here is the point. With consumers, if you create a void in brand belonging, bringing them back in the future is even harder, because consumers are left with a bad impression and a poor experience with your brand. Distribution channels do not work alone. They are there to belong to brands and the audience. The brands become the responsible party in terms of making these channels work, because the Internet is one of the brands' means to reach consumers.

The farther you build the channels of belonging, the more your brand will flourish in the marketplace. The more channels you have, the less you spend on advertising, because the actual consumer will be experiencing your brand and considering all the aspects of brand positioning and factors firsthand.

Distribution or market reach is one of the most vital processes on which a company should exert effort. Even with all the other applicable factors, the simple fact is that the more the product is available to the targeted consumers, the better its chance of performing. Some companies launch their brands with an inefficient geographical distribution plan. How do they expect their brand will perform? Perhaps they are not considering performance at all. The fact is that market reach is one of the basic principles of marketing. For the processes of marketing to work and for a product to become profitable, the company must exert its utmost effort on distribution in order to attain a wider market reach.

Positioning

What is positioning? In a sentence, positioning is the battle for the mind! Al Ries and Jack Trout are the masters, the people who invented the theory of positioning in the world of communication. They pointed out that positioning is the power a brand holds in the minds of the consumer in a very crowded market. Who can say it better than they did? Moreover, who practiced this principle better than President Obama in the last presidential campaign in the United States? President Obama came with a positioning statement: We are here to change the way Washington operates! "Change" was the key word he used in all his communications. He pushed that one word farther than any other candidate to make his point. Eventually, all came to believe that change was to come. Whoever might try to use the word "change" in a subsequent presidential campaign will likely fail because the word is owned in the minds of those who voted for Obama. Positioning is a very simple process. It is what you want to have registered in the audience's minds. Essentially, your position is how you want your audience to know your product and what you stand for. It is the concept or concepts you position in the minds of consumers that differentiate your product from those of your direct competition.

Chapter 6:

BRAND PRODUCT PROFILE

The product profile is the essential determinant of how the brand appears to the consumer. Why is it important how a brand looks, including its name, its colors, and all the other tangibles that are directly associated with the brand profile? Simple. If you don't have these elements incorporated into your brand, you don't have a brand profile. A profile is what builds your brand's character and personality. Neglecting these factors is an invitation to total brand failure. The product will not deliver the message you intend to create in consumers' minds if you don't take your product profile seriously, and you will miss the opportunity for the brand to come to belong to its audience. The power of a brand, when it is tailored methodically according to the prospective target audience, is focused on the segment you plan to attract. Brands are not just names or logos. Brands are like humans; they are like you and me. They need to be managed in order to grow well and thrive.

Colors

With regard to your brand profile, one of the priorities is its colors. There are numerous scientific fundamentals that can play a role when developing a brand, from the colors used to the brand environment, which can then be altered into a brand culture. For example, when you think of black, you may think "expensive." That is a perception on which you can build. Black is an alpha color in the world of communications. When you think of pink, you may think of a Barbie, a girlish color. When you think of orange, a vibrant color, you may think in a cultural sense of a festival, summer, sports, or holiday colors. The corporate blue is always associated with IBM, orange is always associated with Nike, and turquoise is always associated with Tiffany. Today, what sells a brand is the nature of the brand, from its name, its colors, and its personality, to its culture. These are strategies. When you think of red, green, and yellow, these colors are associated with the world of reggae or adopted from the African freedom colors. If you plan to produce a brand targeting African Americans or Africans at large, those three primary colors can represent a whole race. Would you consider those colors to be a win? Yes! Is that a sell? For sure it is! You hit the nail right on the head. The way we desire our colors is the way we seek to live. It is amazing how color communications work. For example, my sorority sister and dear friend Nanette chose earth-tone colors that reflect her love of the outdoors, calmness, and her care for the environment, peace, and love to the world.

Colors should be part of your overall strategy. Every segment of the consumer market is associated with different colors. When you sit and think about the colors you like, you may discover that most of the brands to which you are attached or to which you are relatively close are associated with colors that you like. Each brand color falls in a particular category. For example, black, dark olive green, and fire red represent a prestigious category known as the alpha category. Social colors such as pink, yellow, light green, and regular red are also a category. Evolutionary colors are those that represent space such as gray and silver.

Colors are as important as a brand name, and each segment has a color association that helps create the belonging process to engage with your consumers. You cannot pick just any colors that you like and expect the brand to attain results with your target audience. For example, if you have a multicolor element, this means you are communicating a mass-market brand, because social colors apply to a mass market. When you think through color, it's great how colors work with an audience or how colors can create a drive within a certain audience. This is why I strongly suggest that when choosing a color for your brand, you should consider the process prior to doing so. Each color has a meaning in the mind of prospects; therefore, consider that colors will communicate certain messages that either will or will not attain results for your brand. I will use one example here. What are "corporate" colors? You will find that corporate colors are dark colors; as mentioned above, IBM uses dark blue. Corporate colors communicate the message of "conservative," depending on the industry. My friend Ammar Shata, a financial guru in investment banking, chose a shade of navy blue because it is a color that represents wisdom and leadership, qualities that are at the heart of corporate culture. Others, such as the entertainment industry, could have wild colors, indicating their more social nature. It's important to note here that color connotations can vary by culture. Again, you must know your audience.

Color communications have been divided into four groups: Alpha, Social, Society, and Evolution, with each color having its own meaning behind it. For example, the alpha colors are the expensive brand colors in the eye of the audience. Generally black is an alpha color and reflects prestige and expense. Ferrari fire red is the color of speed and expense; it's also an alpha color. Social colors include yellow, pink, and baby blue, which are the colors of households or the community. Society colors are engaged in a hospital's light green environment or with regard to community service. Evolution colors are space colors like silver and dark gray. You'll usually find them in such places as on your laptop and cell phones.

How important are colors? Well, as do most other things, your colors depend on the product and your target audience. When you think of colors, each one has a meaning, a feeling, and implications, as mentioned above. For now, consider once again the example in which you are trying to launch an energy drink. What color do you imagine the energy to be? Sit a while and think. What is the purpose of the energy drink? What are its core values? Consider these facts, then decide what the colors of the product packaging should be. Consider what your price segment is when you choose colors, because different colors represent certain price segments.

Look

Another consideration is the "look" of your name. There are millions of fonts, but there are standards that can guide you to what font works with your product brand. Not every font will work with every product. For example, various food retail restaurants might use a variety of font types, but each font "looks" somewhat like what the restaurant represents. In other words, Mexican retailers have a certain font type, and steak retailers have a certain font type. If you look at a Mexican brand, usually the font conveys a festive perception. The font is not rigid, has no sharp ends, and may reflect Aztec tribal art. The colors of the brand identity usually reflect the Mexican flag colors or a combination of purples, browns, maroons, yellows—and on rare occasions, blues.

If such a precedent is the case with your product, it's best to follow the rules regarding the public's perception of a font belonging to a particular type of establishment. This is an important distinction: your audience needs to know how your product is different, especially how it's better, but they will tend to distrust difference for its own sake. They have comfort zones, especially for certain product types. You do not have to try to reinvent the wheel. Growth will be slow, but you can still differentiate while staying within certain rules of communications. The value of knowing where your audience's comfort zones are, where they don't welcome difference, and where they might be bored and ready for a change, is another reason getting to know your potential audience is so important.

Shapes: Most retail establishments apply shapes on their logos. If you have not noticed, however, technology brands are generally shape-free; the font type used can often stand alone.

Packaging: When selecting packaging, try your best to create innovative processes within the guidelines of the industry you have selected. Packaging is one of the perceptions that can create a strong impact, but if your product brand packaging is reminiscent of what already exists, you'll need to be ready to fight a belonging war for your product.

Building the brand's profile is a strategic process. Every element mentioned here, and those mentioned below, should be determined by a strategy of communications followed by a strategy of belonging. The principles of this strategy are based on positioning for continuity. The brand profile is part of your total brand building. It's imperative that you understand the inner processes of brand building and the science behind it in order to deliver the kind of impact you seek. The brand profile is the core of your belonging phase with your target audience. All brands need a personality—a character—in order to fulfill their specific purpose to the audience. Look at any human icon who has developed himself into a brand. This person worked on his profile personality and character and later delivered one message through communication regarding what he stands for. He did not change his message every quarter, but delivered one consistent message over time. The same model applies to the profile of your brand. Work on your brand to build the character and personality it takes to engage your audience. Your objective is that the brand will come to belong to your intended target audience. The target audience has expectations, so come to know and strive to meet those expectations as you start the process of the final belonging and the union between the brand and the audience.

Chapter 7:

BRAND PRODUCT PROFILE PART 2: WHAT'S IN A NAME

This is an important enough aspect of the brand profile, and a complicated enough one, that it gets its own chapter. When thinking of a name, think "simple" and select a name that will resonate with your target audience. Don't just choose a name because you like how it sounds. Consider many factors when selecting a name for your brand. Think of your product. What are you trying to sell? To whom? Who is your audience? How is the name associated with your audience? Invariably, the wrong name can undermine many things. For example, you can't position your product in a high-price bracket with a name that will not be attractive as a brand to a wealthier audience. You must also consider what your audience might expect just by reading or hearing the name. Your product's name can also segment your target audience. Some names don't intend to build an association with their target audience; instead, the name may even tend to move an audience away from the product. For example, in the Middle East the two primary languages are Arabic and English, and the use of each language carries its own set of implications with regard to who the target audience is. Some take the brand name as being in alignment with the intended audience's spoken language, and others consider a certain brand whether they speak English or not. Some consumers may take the brand name as an indication that the language of the branding belongs to a certain person with influence or who has a particular place in society. Language also supports self-esteem from low to high in some segments.

Think of the company that produced an energy drink and named it Boom Boom! They were the fourth incoming brand in the market for locally produced energy drinks besides Magic and the other Super Bowl stars. Does the name matter? Let's think about it! How much does a name constitute a difference in the impact of the total brand proposition and perception? The simpler the name, the better chance it has. Meaningful names do matter if the incoming brands are fourth or fifth in the category (they are part of the market share gain). Hertz and Avis are the two big names in rental cars. Where is Alamo? McDonald's, Burger King, and Hardees are the Big Three in fast food burger restaurants. Where is Wendy's or Jack in the Box? When the category expands with more than one brand name, then the latecomers should consider significant names in order to enter the battle for the consumers' minds as a starting point.

So, how do you select a brand name? Ask yourself: To what audience does the brand make a difference? What audience will be most attached emotionally to the belonging processes you build into your brand? After you have converted your idea into a product, the name comes into play as the number one priority.

A name says it all. How do you want your audience to perceive your brand?

Arabic or English?

Create a name that conveys a universal language if you want to ensure your brand is not limited to certain borders. Today's universal language is English. It's a fact we all have to face even if you are a proud Arab. Some names in Arabic can work as universal brands for certain products, such as Diwan or Al Baik, but not all brands and all products. In the case of English, the name can apply to all products and services, depending on the industries. For example, Italian and French names are strong in fashion, but less attractive in other industries. This is due to the fact that these countries have traditionally been strong in building brands that have helped define those industries. Brand names from the United States attract various industries from technology, FMCGs (Fast-Moving Consumer Goods), and even casual fashion apparel.

In choosing a name, it is important to define your long-term goal with your brand name, such as whether the brand is to be regional or global. In the case of Middle Eastern organizations, you must also consider the barriers products might face if they are intended to be known by Arabic names. This consideration has nothing to do with tradition, religion, or culture. If you intend to have your brand name just swim around in the local neighborhood, that's fine. But if it's your ambition to have your brand name extend beyond Arabic-speaking countries, then you should consider the name as a global platform. In the case of Emirates Airlines, it's simple. The name is associated with the United Arab Emirates, the country. So there is a built-in process of belonging in that name. The UAE as a country has positioned itself as a change agent in the Middle East. It represents the change of attaining a modern lifestyle, and the business language of the country has helped to spread its name to the rest of the world. In this case, if it works for the country, then it works for the airlines. In the case of Ithhad Airlines, does its name and its context have the same impact as those of Emirates? This airline has positioned itself as a luxury carrier, but the name is hard for many people to remember unless somehow Ithhad hammers people through over-advertising. The name works for outbound flights from Abu Dhabi, but not for inbound flights. For English speakers, it unfortunately resembles the words "it had," a phrase that doesn't convey anything good, if it conveys anything at all. It's thus a name that works only with those who are associated with the Arabic language or those who have experienced the brand. Names can belong to an audience, but when a brand goes global, then the brand must be so unique in its product or service that a name such as Ithhad or Al Jazeera can belong to a non-Arab speaking audience.

In the midst of the second gulf war in Iraq, Al Jazeera, the Arabic news channel, hit the global platform due to its controversial broadcasting, and the brand, while it automatically belonged to the Arab world, was still heard clearly in every nation on the earth. For example, when Al Jazeera focused on the task of covering the Gulf War from the Arab perspective, it stirred up controversy such that some of the channel's coverage was picked up by CNN and FOX, giving Al Jazeera a platform whereon to expose its name not only to the Western world but all across the globe. It didn't hurt that the name was sufficiently catchy that it registered easily and came to belong to households. The power of a name is such that it can sometimes move fast in any language when it has support based on being the intentional agent of controversy or when it moves in an opposite direction from its competitors in a way that people are ready for. That is what Al Jazeera did.

The Good, the Bad, and the Ugly

Names are magic for brands, and names are intimately related to the strategy of belonging. If you wish for your brand to belong, think of the right name that will communicate the brand to the world of your target audience. Japanese firms have learned this lesson from the past, as have Koreans. But names such as Hyundai and Kia have worked over their competitors only as they worked in conjunction with pricing factors. We all know that South Asia intended to have long names for their products, but the names by which they are known were created to be English-friendly and to serve as prospective names on global platforms. A name is as important as other parts of the branding strategy when it comes to a brand. The question that you should ask at this point is, "Would I consider that my brand's name is part of the total strategy?" The answer is clear: Yes, it is! A name has an impact, but it is also something that the mind can easily reject. A name has a great role as part of your overall brand strategy. Many firms study names and conduct research prior to naming a brand. They consider the long-term life of the brand and how the name can be sustainable. The right name for the brand will be easy for the target audience to identify as belonging in their lives.

Throughout my experiences, I have encountered many names of companies or even FMCGs and have wondered what in the world the chairman was thinking when he settled on the name of his product with his marketing department. How long did he want to travel with this name, and how did he assess the impact of the name? So many questions go through my head when I see such names as Boom Boom! for an energy drink. This product was a complete flop from the name itself all the way to what the company intended to do with the rest of the products. Also, what about a name such as Health Plus Corner? Would you ever name a place that sells items related to health—one that operates much like a supermarket and features chocolate ice cream and a restaurant—something like Health Plus Corner? Wow! What comes to my mind is: what corner are they selling with a name like that? I have witnessed so many names in the Middle East, such as Diamond portable drinking water, and have been amazed how people can think a name like that can elevate a brand when instead the name sends out the wrong impression. A name has to be well thought-out prior to other portions of the strategy so that the total communications for a brand will create an impact. Meaningless names with only a few letters can also have a great impact based on what the product is and what the prospective brand communications will be. Recently, we have even seen created names that a firm owns become words in the dictionary.

Names, Ego, and the Problem of Getting Good Advice

I don't always know what people who go with bad names were thinking, but I have some ideas. So, at this point, let me inject what may be some important ideas concerning the relationship of the naming process with the ego and with human emotion— advice that may apply to other aspects of the brand profile as well. Naming your product, or naming anything, comes before you as an emotionally charged enterprise. Names have an extraordinary importance in every culture that I know of. Names and naming appear to be a universally fundamental and vitally important part of the human experience. Think of all the proverbs and references to the value of a name, or about preserving the integrity or honor of a name. Think of all the ceremonies and rituals we attach to naming, from ceremonies applying names to newborn babies, to smashing bottles on the hulls of new ships. All that is good and argues for the importance of a name, but it also comes with a set of challenges.

The problem the emotional significance of naming brings about is twofold. First, in all the excitement and ego investment of naming a new product, your emotional attachment to a certain name can blind you to its flaws. I don't mean anything insulting when I say "ego investment." I'm speaking of ego in terms of the core of your identity. Part of the process of naming means that you become identified with the thing you've named. That is to say, it sort of becomes a part of you, and likewise there's a piece of you in it. In this process, you may get attached to a name or become excited about a name idea, or to put it more specifically, your identification with a name as its creator may lead you to see all its good points and to not only fail to consider its downsides but to actively and aggressively resist criticism, or even resist a simple, thoughtful process of evaluation.

At this point, your name attachment gives rise to a second problem with regard to naming. People are sensitive creatures. People you ask about your new product name (or other brand profile features) will sense your attachment to it, and being the socially driven creatures they are, they will likely take as their first priority in the conversation what they see as their responsibility to make you happy. This means that they will be inclined to say they agree with you about your name idea, even if they truly have reservations, at least initially, because they like you and want you to feel good, as well as because intervening in that naming process, with its links to the sacred, is something of a taboo.

This fact about the dynamics of conversation is a truth you may want to get used to, by the way: for most people, the social aspect of a conversation very often trumps the informational aspect of a conversation. That is to say, what people want you to feel as a result of a conversation is more important to them than the conversation's truth content. Does this amount to a form of polite lying? Perhaps so. At any rate, when people communicate with you they will have as their first priority keeping you happy. This is not just me talking—studies have shown this to be the case. Moreover, this is not just a matter of people fudging when they compliment your product name or your hairstyle. People build their entire identities, or more accurately, have them built, through this social dynamic of conversation. Political affiliations, aesthetic preferences, religious alignment—all these things may be primarily formed through the social interplay that is conversation, and not through any intellectual process. This is to say, if you want to know what someone thinks, check with the beliefs of the people he or she talks to. Change who someone talks to on an ongoing basis, and you change what he or she thinks. This is another reason why you can't simply think up a product and find a way to make it belong to a particular audience. That audience operates under its own set of rules, which have been formed by the way they interact; as an outsider, you have no power to change what they like or don't like, or practically none.

At any rate, this fact of our social condition is why it is truly a gift to have someone in your organization who's sufficiently confident with you—or willing to be sufficiently rude, depending on how you look at it—to be able to summon the courage to tell you the truth, even when the truth may hurt. If you don't have a person who you are completely certain is willing to take that risk with you, that's when it's time to bring in a consultant. Even then, you'll still need to make sure that the consultant you hire is somebody who earns his or her money by giving clients valuable advice, whether it's something they want to hear or not. Do not make the mistake of bringing in somebody who makes quick cash by kissing up to clients and telling them what they want to hear. The more scientific you can make the naming process, the better, as long as that process is combined with creativity and vision, precisely because it's a subject that requires systematic effort to detach from emotionally.

Apart from the natural ego involvement that comes along with assigning a name, some companies and brand owners have the good, old-fashioned kind of ego commonly called arrogance. They think they can name their product whatever they like and make their audience like it. To put it simply, those people are mistaken, and their brands are in trouble unless they find a way to fix the root of the problem, which isn't their bad product name. It's their careless attitude and their lack of consideration for their consumers, both of which bode ill for their future in business.

Names for Dot Coms

It seems as if names are always already taken in the dot com world. Names with few letters are almost impossible to get, which is why new brands often attain two names for their dot com or use a dash. At times, I have even seen numbers included. The following question always pops into my head when words are registered as brand names: "Will a person remember the dot com when it includes a dash, numbers, and a million other extensions?" Never! You should exert the effort to ensure your brand name and your dot com destination are the same, without extensions, in large part because the Internet is one of your major communication channels. For example, I know of a health club in the Middle East that owns a brand name. However, that brand name is a bit extended on the dot com destination, a situation that is likely to result in confusion and misplaced searches. The dot com is part of your overall branding process. With your dot com, you are trying to create reach between your target audience and your physical location.

I have also seen a product that could be branded "GIUT" with the dot com name of *www.guit4-KSA.com*. This is just an example, but if the name is available to be branded as GUIT, the dot com destination should be part of the reach and part of the overall processes of branding. That being the case, how could *www.guit4-ksa.com* be remembered as the dot com name for this product? It will never happen. In considering whether the dot com name will work, you must first plan to take a global prospective. Then, forget being a ".com.sa" or ".com.eg" or something similar. This designation will only localize the perception of your brand. Second, when you select a name for your brand, consider the importance of the "dot." Search the Internet and determine if the brand name is available before deciding on a name. Once you make sure the name before the "dot com" is available, consider legally protecting your name locally and globally. By doing so, you will be able to build a brand name that is more secure.

Chapter 8:

BRAND PRODUCT PROFILE PART 3: EMOTION, PLACEMENT, PACKAGING

The Sensory and Emotional Content of a Brand

When thinking of the sensory and emotional content of a brand, think of the emotions of your family or loved ones. Emotions apply to brands because all brands are like humans. They live and they engage people based on their emotional attributes. Considering that consumers use their five senses when engaging with a brand, segments will differ with regard to emotional impacts. When speaking to an upper-income segment of the audience, the emotional impact of the brand must be there in the product profile in order to have an impact on the brand environment. Some brand owners take this subject lightly. They may believe that the design is the only point that attracts the audience and grasps their attention to help form an intention to buy the brand. That is totally wrong! From the name and the brand profile to the product line, the brand culture and communications are the strongest points that create emotional brand impact. If you disregard emotional factors, then the brand process of making a product belong to an audience is nil.

Remember—every human sensation of like or dislike sends messages to the brain in the process of buying a product. The brain is the central consideration, but it can be overpowered by emotions and blinded to the price factor (which actually could be an obstacle if the brand price is too expensive, however). When thinking of how you create the process of belonging to the audience, it all starts from the name and profile and so on. But one very important factor in determining the impact you make is how you communicate the purpose of or the reason for the product to various audiences and what media you use to communicate those aspects of your product. Words and visuals are two very powerful elements in creating interest and reach. These must be followed by the right deliverables as product brands to the audience. Emotional content allows the brand to live longer throughout all the phases through which the brand will live. If the brand misses its emotional link, it will start its decline in the life of the brand process. For many reasons, brand management needs to maintain brand consistency in terms of its emotional deliverables. It is dangerous to change the emotional communication of your brand for any other reason than to benefit your brand. If you have the opportunity to experience luxury brands, you will find that you encounter an emotional experience from the time you walk in the door of the store—or the time you log on to a site—to the time you leave.

Product Placement

Product placement is the employees' personal connection that links the brand to the customer. This can be a simple gesture or service. For example, during one of my trips to Hong Kong, I had an incredible and unforgettable emotional experience. As soon as I arrived at the hotel, an employee greeted me and guided me to the front desk to check in. While I was waiting, one of the guest services employees approached me, started entertaining me, and invited me to enjoy a refreshment. I'm a seasoned traveler, but all this personal attention elevated the brand in my heart, and now the brand belongs to me as a customer. This is an example of a successful effort to create a sense of emotional belonging.

A second example involves an airline I was flying. For the entire trip, the flight attendants made sure that they focused their personal attention on each guest and attended to their requests. That quality of service left me wanting not only to fly again on that airline, but to actually make sure that wherever I go, I will book through that airline if doing so is logical. When the times comes to fly, my excitement at seeing the plane parked at the gate holds a special feeling in my heart and keeps the brand in my mind as the most respected.

The other factor to which you should pay attention is not the luxury you plan to provide, but the emotional attributes you plan to add to your brand. I have flown on other airlines that use the word "luxury," but their service was seriously missing the emotional touch. Emotions are very vital in the life of the brand. For the brand to interact and attain results, brand owners must recognize this process as fundamentally important in creating a cash flow for their business.

Product Packaging

Remember, a product's packaging will be your customer's first sensory encounter with your product. In a sense, it often represents your first chance to make a sensory, and thus an emotional, connection with your audience. At times, firms can tend to disregard the importance of the process of selecting packaging and just accept whatever is available. Sometimes, this "any-old-packaging" decision replicates what already exists for other brands. This sort of non-decision does not do your brand any favors. In reality, however, a brand category tends to replicate packaging styles for almost every brand. The differentiation factor comes in the design and brand profile. But what happens if you find a way to do innovative packaging? Differentiating your brand can spring not only from the brand profile, but the packaging as well. With unique packaging, not to mention what the product itself delivers, the brand will tend to stand out within the category. Packaging is a very important process in ensuring a long-living strategy. It seems a minor consideration, but if this factor is neglected, everything else about your brand could fail.

We all have experienced a day in our lives when a certain kind of brand was launched in a certain category. We may have considered not only the brand profile, but also the packaging, which contributes to its strong or even dominant competitive power. In this case, such a brand has moved completely away from the competition and created something new for others to follow.

I remember very well a dairy product brand in the milk line that came out strong when it was launched. This was in Egypt back in 1999. The owner of the newly launched brand was well aware that he was entering a very tight UHT long-life category of milk. Still, the company decided to move away from the carton pack to a plastic bottle pack, which I thought was a very innovative aspect to add to this brand's profile. When the brand launched, I observed its strong hold. Consumer curiosity drove them to the product on the shelf. So, while we all know it's just milk, the perception strategy drove the brand at great speed off the shelves at launch even without an advertising campaign. The impact here was the differentiating factor that added the element of the belonging of the product to a new segment, with good reach and the ability to penetrate the market. Several months later, the plastic bottle packaging had created a new category for others to follow. Other dairy product companies entered the category with their own products. They had the same brand name as the old carton UHT milk. But in their cases the companies ended up being second and fifth in the category because the packaging was owned in the hearts of consumers by the first owner. This is an excellent example of how powerful packaging can be integral to the life of a brand. Have you ever sat around with friends or family, and when they mentioned a brand, they tended to mention its packaging and color? This sort of thing happens because certain brands—if they have unique packaging—carry a different perception from other brands that exist in that category. In this case, word of mouth comes into play such that others will begin to seek out the experience of that brand. The pull factor is working in that case to create a growing population that will follow your brand.

Consider how many packages we have seen and how many brands were effective from their launch because of packaging or other emotional elements. This can be the case when a brand can react to consumers' expectations and perceptions based on how the brand owner created the brand. The success of any brand depends on the consumers' initial reactions to engaging with the product. If that reaction is positive, the brand will experience sustained growth. If the emotional and belonging elements are totally out of the picture, then what you can expect as a brand owner is failure, because the product does not connect with the consumer.

This process can be characterized as a two-way relationship. The brand must meet expectations—both the brand owner's and the consumer's. But it is more important to ensure the consumer's expectations are placed above the brand owner's expectations in order for the brand to deliver its purpose. In terms of marketing and brand design, the old adage is truer than ever: the customer is always right.

Throughout my experience in marketing, I have met many hardheaded business owners who determine the life of the brand not based on experience, but instead based on personal satisfaction. These owners are driven by their egos and their claim that they are the mind behind this great brand. Unfortunately, the result in most of these cases is the failure to achieve their personal purposes, precisely because they simply decide what to do at their own risk. Such posturing in the Middle East falls apart when it comes to marketing and what the brand should deliver to consumers. My hope is that these cases will diminish in the future so the region can witness serious growth and move away from our repetitive lifestyle of being followers rather than leaders. Unfortunately, we see business owners invest in wasted time and money, disregarding the most important elements that will help them attain cash flow. Such orthodoxy is embedded deep in our business society. Change is something that creates fear. Owners fight against this fear in order to proceed with their personal and egotistical goals and to maintain the image of a certain sort of man-in-charge kind of machismo.

Chapter 9:

BRAND COMMUNICATION PART 1: INTERNAL BRAND PROCESSING

What do we really mean by brand communication? Who delivers brand messages? Such questions quite often enter the minds of brand owners in the Middle East region. Unfortunately, companies that are inadequately prepared to carry out brand communication enter the market to deliver such sensitive information. Who controls the processes? Some companies ignore the credentials of ad agencies just because they offer a "good" price. Others consider those credentials precisely because they are keenly aware of the importance of their brand and don't want to make a mistake at this crucial stage. The road is filled with potholes of confusion for most clients, especially those who have the least experience in brand-building processes or total strategies. In my previous book, *Eccentric Marketing*, I argued that many can say they are skilled in graphic design and add that claim to their marketing services. The industry is undermined by improperly understanding the policies and bylaws that such an industry should uphold. Another problem in the industry hereabouts is that there is currently no association that oversees the functionality of individual companies. Most companies can claim anything they want as a service and not even be categorized. Such a miasma of exalted or false claims and underperformance must be fixed right now, for it will only pose more difficulties in the years to come.

There are many industries and individual companies that should not only strive to better identify their industry, but also the category to which they belong so that they can achieve professional focus. For example I might be in the fast food industry, which is general, but be focused in the burger category. In this way the brand could belong to the category, and for the audience who are burger lovers and appreciate and know about the burger category, the brand could have a better chance to be easily identified and thus to come to belong to the audience.

The process of brand communications has two components: internal branding and external branding. The initial phase is internal branding, which means that every employee within the organization understands the total brand process from the beginning to the end. Internal branding helps all levels of management understand the brand life and the expected deliverables to the external audience. Internal branding also serves the purpose of relieving the company's brand operations of any confusion in the future in terms of how departments link processes. For example, marketing and finance departments frequently fall apart in their operations due to misunderstandings. External branding is the most important aspect of branding. It is the life of the company and encompasses the conduct of the whole process of delivering the product to a target audience. We can even go so far as to say it's the reason for the company's existence. External branding processes differ in important ways from internal branding processes. External branding focuses on communicating to a larger audience through one message regarding the brand identity, its profile, its reason for existing, and its movement. It is a single message via brand positioning that uses the processes of content and visual representations to communicate.

Internal Processing Means Being in a Relationship with Employees

Internal brand processing ensures that employees of the organization are well aware of the brand and its reasons for existing. Many factors apply here. One of the core factors encompasses not only the stakeholders' knowledge of the product, but also the love employees express toward the brand and by which the brand comes to belong in the lives of employees at all levels. You may witness employees who work for a reputable firm express strong pride for the brands for which they work. This pride and attachment is expressed through self-confidence regarding their company's performance or the brand itself. Look at major reputable firms such as IBM, Microsoft, Unilever, and Procter & Gamble. These companies have built corporate brand understanding and product lines through regular and constructive training regarding the brand and its corporate purpose. Internal branding also helps cement employee relationships. The Human Resource department or a cooperative service should always be alert to opportunities to implement further training that will elevate internal branding through the marketing department. For this reason and many others, it is essential to outline the simple steps that help employees understand the brand.

Brand Functionality

Brand functionality is the process of taking an idea and developing the brand's personality, character, and life. At times, for various reasons, the head of marketing and corporate management withhold this sort of information from other levels of management and rank-and-file employees. I believe that this is the most critical mistake that they can make. Employees being trusted to possess company information is not merely based on their having signed a contract. If corporate management truly wants to build the brand, that brand must belong to every employee in the firm.

The most important functionality of which to make your employees aware with regard to your brand is in terms of brand positioning, its personality, and the brand's emotional attributes. One of the primary benefits of informing your employees of brand positioning is that employees then become the foot solders that sell your brand to the public. The process of how they communicate the brand to their friends, neighbors, and the public at large is something that training can help manage. Just communicating the basic "do's and don'ts" of brand positioning to your employees can make them effective messengers. The other factor to communicate to your employees is the brand personality. What is the brand personality? What is the culture of the brand that is built around it? It is essential that employees know the ins and outs of the personality and the culture so that they, too, can live the experience of the brand and come to appreciate it. When they have processed the product as a brand that belongs to them and when they are proud to work for your company, you have effective messengers.

The process of exhibiting the brand positioning, personality, and culture to your employees also means creating the emotional attributes that you expect the employees to exhibit toward the company and the brand. The employee of any firm should understand well the brand positioning of the firm and the corporate culture so that they can be more effective advocates of the brand. In the long term they are the walking PR agents of their brands. For example, consider an employee that works for a large company with global offices and a great reputation. That employee is so proud of where he works that he uses the brand name often to bolster his own reputation: I work for JP Morgan, I work for Bank of America, I work for Armani, and so on. The brand's external reputation and internal human relations have produced a valuable PR soldier on all fronts. The brand is in action.

In some ways, employees are more effective advocates than marketers because in terms of their perceived reliability on the part of the public, the public will perceive that they aren't getting paid to spread the word about the company and the product—they are doing so because they believe in the company and the product. As with the distinction between advertising and word of mouth that we discussed above, that's the difference between whether the audience attributes an intrinsic or an extrinsic motivation to the employee's message. That is, is he saying this because he believes it, or because he gets paid to say it? Of course, on that scale consumers are the best PR agents of all for the product. But employees can be immensely valuable in this regard.

As the owner, the brand life depends on you, and the emotional content you set for your brand and your company is processed through your employees. Employees can deliver excitement as an organization in working together and delivering the ultimate goal.

Not convinced? Let's talk about the downside of not investing in employees' involvement with the brand. First, let's talk about downsides with regard to whether you decide to share information with your employees. The thing you need to be aware of here is that information is a two-way street. Information is a resource, an asset, a commodity. If you don't share that commodity in your organization, you can't expect anyone to share that commodity with you. You as the owner set the tone of the organization in terms of information sharing. If you set a precedent whereby information is hoarded, you're setting yourself up for a fall. Why?

Of all the information sources available to you, employees are perhaps the most important. They are on the front lines—they know what's happening on the ground, so to speak. They know where production may be hitting snags. They get feedback from customers that management could easily be unaware of. Often, they themselves may even be members of your target audience and therefore be able to produce valuable consumer information firsthand. Closing off that avenue of information by setting an information-hoarding tone for your organization can thus have devastating consequences. How information gets shared, or not, within a company can thus be a fundamental determinant of how well the company does.

Second, there's the issue of morale. I realize this is a marketing book, not a management book, but bear with me—I'll connect the dots in a moment. If employees feel that they are stakeholders, if they feel that they're looped in to the branding process and that their needs and feelings are important to you, they will work better than if they feel they are simply being used. Attending to employees' needs, training them, sharing information with them, all these are proven ways—and by that I mean empirically proven ways—of improving employee morale and thus improving the company.

Here's where employee morale and information come back to marketing. Yes, if employees are happy and are involved in the branding process, only happy customers can do more as unpaid PR agents than employees. But yes, the converse is true. If employees are unhappy, nobody except unhappy customers can do more to damage your brand. Remember, employees are the front line of your interaction with customers. It's not just that happy, informed employees are good for your business, although they certainly are, from the way they help production to the way they can help improve the product and the brand to the way they treat customers—it's also that unhappy, disfranchised employees have the power to sink your business to the bottom of the seas of commerce.

I know of a company that did not conduct any internal branding processes or help employees understand the purposes and the goals of the brand. The organization became divided and failed to deliver due to an environment of … well, "hatred" is not too strong a word … that resulted within the organization. Employees disliked even working for the firm. This cascade of hate is always a problem that reflects on the brand's functionality. Have you ever eaten at a restaurant that is branded within a chain or visited a fashion retail outlet and disliked how you were treated? Perhaps if you did, you also saw an employee behind the counter being careless with his job. These are reasons for brand failure, because the management never thought of team building or brand building. The owner or manager never thought to instill the emotional benefits of the brand in employees to help sustain brand growth. We all know some of the most important things are invisible and only tangible through the emotions we observe and give. The management that neglects the importance of internal brand building is management that has no clear vision of a long-term brand strategy or even of the firm's goals.

Brand Deliverables

Brand deliverables are the results that the brand should deliver to an organization's employees and what the management should expect as a committed team supports and delivers the total brand objectives. In this case, management and employees hold various expectations of how the brand benefits them at the corporate level. These are benefits and rewards that the managers and employees expect from the corporation and the brand as they become foot soldiers for the product. Ideally, corporate management should understand the long-term benefits of the brand and reward managers and employees with financial benefits and other rewards (including the use of the brand, depending on the industry). For example, as a manager or employee your part of a luxury hotel chain is key to keeping the brand consistent via all sources of contact with guests. A discount or special rate should therefore apply to employees, along with their families, for the purposes of promoting the brand. Other rewards can also come along, but the nature of the rewards depends on how successful the brand is.

The belonging reach here with regard to deliverables has to do with the employees' expectations of rewards for their efforts to make the brand work. Just as the brand has to meet its audience's expectations of the product or service, in the same way, for the brand to come along well, it must also meet the employees' expectations in terms of rewards. This relational link keeps the firm alive in harmony and positions it to reach its strategic goals over both the short and long term. Such efforts are, unfortunately, almost non-existent in the Middle East. For firms that plan to reach a global platform, their expectation is for employees to deliver strong brand messages but not to expect rewards for these deliverables.

This characteristic of Middle Eastern companies to neglect the interests of their employees is unfortunate not just for the employees, but also for the firms. A company that experiences high employee turnover is a company that is undermining the life of its own brand. The processes of the human resources department and the administration should be designed to make sure that all employees are living the brand and harmonizing their experience at work to instill a great liking for their organization. For example, look at employees that work for major reputable firms around the world— IBM, JP Morgan, Microsoft, and the rest. These employees are not only proud of how reputable their firms are but also proud of how the firm treats them. Opportunities are there for their growth on both a career and a personal level. These factors of employee consideration are essential if the organization is to believe that they have a model to measure their expectations concerning employees' deliverables. Employees belong to a firm, and a firm belongs to employees.

Pride and Emotion in the Brand

Employees' love for the brand and the company for which they work can help achieve excellent results, helping to ensure the firm's financial success and delivering on its overall strategies and goals. An employee who understands the brand's purpose and value will "wear" the brand with pride based on his emotional connection to the firm, if that firm has provided him with benefits and growth opportunities. Emotions are an important factor within the organization in order for the brands to resonate with consumers. A capacity for delivering expectations, pride, and emotions are connected to establishing the emotion of love in the heart of your organization. This pride in the company can be manifested through the hearts of its employees.

To illustrate my point, I will provide an opposite example of what I'm talking about. I have witnessed several companies that apply a strategy of instilling hard-core fear in their managers and employees through the use of threats and deductions in pay without any consideration for contractual agreements, policies, and procedures. Such companies operate under the belief that such an approach will motivate employees and managers to produce. On the contrary, my dear readers. Such an approach can only serve to bring the company and the brand down. Many companies in the Middle East unfortunately apply this theory, and it has caused the firm either to completely fail or has forced their employees to seek new job opportunities. The question becomes this: how can the firm sustain itself if employees are always looking for other job opportunities? What's the best that can happen? Those who have experienced this kind of tragedy or who have caused their company to flop can best answer these questions.

The essential processes of emotion and care are part of your firm's internal branding process. Your HR department must be active in creating the sort of emotional attributes for the firm that will invite the organization's employees to feel that they belong to the firm and work to build upon the firm's expectations. For example: how many CEOs hope that their employees will walk out of the workplace and be proud of where they work? I believe all of them. How does this happen? It all starts from the CEO and his direct instructions to the HR and the administration divisions on how to provide for the employees' growth opportunities and benefits. As important as it is that the brand is communicated externally, it is also imperative that the brand be well communicated internally so that the belonging processes works as whole.

The Brand's Belonging

How could you work somewhere where you feel that you don't belong, but rather that you have merely accepted the job because of the salary? Who is responsible for assessing what kind of employees should be hired so that they can have more of a sense of purpose than that and be infused with the corporate culture, even at the entry level? The firm that plans to belong to the market and have a great impact should initially work on a proper foundation so that the employees hired possess certain criteria that mesh well with the company's industry outlook. When an employee feels he belongs to a certain corporation, he automatically adapts himself to the new experience. It's easier for the firm to develop a sense of internal brand belonging if the employees they hire believe in the company's strategies and positioning. We all belong somewhere, just as it is important for the brand to belong in the lives of the audience. It is also critically important that the brand belong in the lives of the employees that represent the company publicly.

The brand-belonging process in employees' hearts will never take place until the initial processes are built, however, and the company implements human resource policies and procedures to that end. Employees must be ready to sign on and accept their duties with open hearts. When that happens, the employee is not merely clocking in for drudgery; he is taking steps to adapt himself and his feelings in order to serve the company with pride.

Chapter 10:

BRAND COMMUNICATION PART 2: EXTERNAL BRAND PROCESSING

Internal to External Branding

What will external branding to the market mean if the company's internal branding is not in place? This is a simple question, and the simple answer is that neglecting internal branding is the beginning of failure. The process of external branding means publicizing the brand identity and its tagline so that it registers in the minds of the target audience. The external branding core value for deliverables lies in good positioning, tag lines, using consistent brand colors, ensuring a strong brand culture, and infusing the media and content used to deliver the brand message with a sense of purpose. Each of the above elements is part of the bigger branding picture delivered to the audience to allow them to understand the purpose and culture of your brand. External branding to your audience is more than just public relations and advertising. If the core foundation of the communications strategy is not drafted effectively, then your communication will be all over the place, sending out different messages, some of them unintended. Such a problem occurs quite often in the reality of our marketplace, because companies fly from product development straight to advertising without establishing brand planning, belonging processes, and cultural development.

Positioning

Brand positioning lies in the process of establishing the marketing mix. Managers should think carefully and thoroughly about brand positioning and how they want the target audience to perceive the brand. The processes of positioning support the quest for belonging in terms of identifying the audience so that the brand can live in the hearts of the audience. Positioning has natural laws that firms should apply as prescribed by Al Ries and Jack Trout. The brand positioning in the minds of prospects cannot be ignored, because position is what differentiates the brand and moves it away from its competition. Positioning is the art of finding ways to have the brand essence live in the minds of the audience, the art of having the brand thoroughly felt and perceived, and of having it directed to stand for something such that it will be known for its essence.

The strength of positioning is when the brand holds a place in the prospects' minds as the only brand for a copy machine, toothpaste and so on. Perfect examples of companies that have managed this task well abound. Xerox, when it first launched, was positioned as a copy machine manufacturer and held that position in the mind of its prospects. To this day people often don't say, "photocopy it"; they say, "Xerox it for me." That's how powerful the brand is and has been. When Federal

Express launched it was Federal Express, the first overnight delivery service, and as soon as the audience grew to know it as fast or even overnight, which was the firm's positioning, that positioning led the audience to believe that when you say "FedEx" it means "overnight"—as in, "FedEx this to Jeddah for me." Years later, Federal Express actually changed its name to FedEx in recognition of the name its customers had given it. That is the power of positioning.

A theme that has been running through what we've said here needs to have explicit attention drawn to it once again at this point. That is, positioning and some of these other concepts can be handled in the abstract for a run-of-the-mill product. However, the best way to position your product is to make a really great product. Finding something new to do that everyone needs and wants and finding something you can do so well or in such a new way that nobody else stands a chance are the best ways to position your brand. Yes, you can find an audience after you've made your product, but better yet, you can know your audience so well that you get a sense for what they need and want, come up with your product based on those wants and needs, and act quickly to give it to them before anyone else can. In other words, the best way to position your brand is to do what you do really, really well. Even given the predominance of English in global marketing, is it still your ambition to found an Arabic brand name that's known and honored worldwide? That can happen! But only when the product so branded is the best of its kind. I imagine there are lots of American skaters who would be happy to ride a "Fahd" skateboard, for instance, if it were the best skateboard made. Then, however, the honor of the success of the brand would be conferred based on its excellence, not based merely on someone's cultural or linguistic preference. And guess what? Honor based on excellence is the only true honor. In other words, I guess I'm saying, "Don't skip the earlier chapters in order to read this one!"

Tagline

Despite the importance of positioning, most companies ignore that vital step and proceed directly to developing a tagline. Taglines capture the heart of positioning. Your positioning is presented in the tagline so that customers can understand what you stand for through two or three powerful words. The tagline is not something you come up with in order to look trendy or to have something that represents the brand icon. Instead, it works through the brand positioning such that both are well embedded in the brand's identity. I have witnessed people use the word "quality" in their tag line. How can you position quality? Your positioning should be what evolves from the brand to meet the expectations of your target audience. "Quality" in a tag line has no connection to belonging. It's a statement that the owners of the brand make regarding their own perception, not the perception of the audience. Of course companies say their products are quality; what else are they going to say? "Mediocrity"? You may as well not say anything at all as to say something banal and expected like "quality."

For example, I know of a beverage company that had more than twenty product lines across a range of categories. Its tagline indicated its products were "your local beverage." My question is this: if every brand out there is a local brand, then what differentiates this brand from other local competitors? Product brand lines and categories might as well have been neglected in this case. But, you may say, the company that produces the beverages is positioned as a local company. My simple response is this: does the audience experience the company or the brand? Certainly, the brands should be positioned and the tagline created to support the process of belonging. This process should apply to the brands and not the companies. One of this company's brands had words on the can that simply said, "Top Quality." Such a statement is not only an uninteresting claim; it is also an unfounded claim. Who is going to believe the company's integrity in its suggestion that the product is top quality unless the product is experienced? It would then be the audience's perception that the product is top quality and not merely the perception of the company geniuses who underestimated the power of the audience. Taglines are part of the brand essence. They reflect on the brand positioning and should be able to describe the brand positioning in only a few words. Take, for an example, this test. Think about what would be the brand positioning of the following brands based on their taglines: Nike (just do it), Pepsi (new generation), and Starbucks (third place from home). Think about it and see if you can discover why in the case of Starbucks I stated the positioning for you and not the tagline.

Brand Colors

Colors should not just be a reflection of your tastes based on your perceptions as the owner of a business. The colors you use in relation to brand communication, including through print or online media, must work through scientific analysis of the colors that apply to each industry and each target audience. In this way, the core message may be aligned with other elements of your positioning. Each color carries a certain array of meanings, and certain colors apply differently to certain segments. For example, we all know that red is a retail color. But at the same time, we all know that red and yellow represent lower-priced factors in terms of price strategy. Another example is that you always see yellow and black on construction or industrial brands. This exhibits that these colors are familiar ones for that category and for those prospective customers. What happens when you reinvent the wheel in terms of your color palette, unless it's something that is a totally innovative product that is being launched for the first time and belongs squarely in a new category? By trying to reinvent the color aspect of communication, you will stunt the brand's growth until the colors are established effectively through advertising. You can imagine the cost of that! For these reasons and many others, I would consider reinventing colors or creating new colors only when you are certain that you have an innovative brand with innovation appeal.

Many factors apply in terms of color communications. In the Middle East, brand colors and communication apply only if a business owner likes them and wishes to add the value of his own taste or even his relatives' preferences. Such a situation is very consistent in the region, and yet Middle Eastern business owners will not accept the processes of effective brand belonging in order for their brands to flourish. I have witnessed attitudes like this many times, and the result was always catastrophic. Can you imagine a scenario in which business owners admit their mistakes and ask their marketing department or advertising agency to redo the whole thing? How could that possibly work? The consumer has already experienced the negative impact of a poorly planned branding implementation. How in the world is the business owner going to change his mind again and still have his brand flourish? Many business owners think such a thing is easy to do. I'm here to tell you, "No!" The rules of belonging mean that the way you engage customers on an emotional level can have a negative or a positive impact. The consumer's bad experience with the brand is a negative impact. Instead of the brand belonging to the audiences' hearts, it spirals into the process of dislike, or if you like, "negative belonging." The perfect example in the context of the Middle East is when the CEO or family business owner sits around with his family and friends and decides on the colors of the brand and avoids the expertise of the agency. The simple appraisal of what's going on in such a scenario is that the owner seeks to satisfy his no-good ego over the brand's goal to belong to the audience, which will make or break the brand's success. When objectives are not stated in the heart of processes, the result is usually a blunder.

The Brand Culture

The brand culture is how the brand represents itself in its cultural form. Think of two primary movements in the '60s and '70s, which were the Hippie and Rasta movements. These two cultural movements made an impact by embracing the importance of peace and equality in the world. These two movements each generated many brands that attached themselves to the same cultural philosophy. For example, there was a brand called Living Colors that followed the Rasta movement. The colors of these two cultural phenomena moved through many brands. For example, it's easy to remember that red, green, and yellow represented the Rasta movement. And, think of Harley Davidson! What a fascinating brand culture this company presents as based on the biker culture that emerged in the '60s. Harley practically owns the colors black and orange as the dominant colors of bikers' clothing.

Brand cultures support the brand in terms of sales and underlie the most significant processes of belonging. With a strong culture, a brand can become almost a cult, characterized by pride in the brand and the utmost, deeply felt culture of emotional belonging. Brand culture has one of the strongest impacts on supporting a brand and its continuity. The culture also supports the firm's employees standing strong when presenting the brand to the public audience. Many brands have a strong internal brand culture, which sets the example for creating an external brand culture. When employees love their jobs and their company, this attachment becomes a strong belonging factor by which the brand can come to enjoy a sense of belonging both internally and externally. In terms of establishing a brand culture, the process involves developing a certain standard for a way of life in terms of corporate conduct that will sustain the company's growth. Culture also helps to grow the brand internally and externally such that the brand creates a certain way of life for its audience to which they can belong en masse. Brand culture is a series of associated ideas, images, and beliefs that the brand embraces and that society can embrace through identifying with certain shared beliefs and thoughts related to the brand and its deliverables. In considering this sort of identification, I believe that the power of belonging rests in the shared values represented by a brand culture. How can we intend to have audiences follow our brands if we don't intend to build a brand culture that they will experience and live through? As an example, look at Harley Davidson. The product is a motorbike, but the brand sells a lifestyle and a culture. Harley Davidson expects its audience to *live* when riding a bike. The merchandising, the music, the unmistakable sound of the V-twin engine, and much else besides will be a part of the culture, so that the customer purchases the product not just to have a means of transportation but in order to be able to live that experience—to be part of that culture.

Brand Elements

When we think of visual communications for the brand other than the logo, what you use for your brand should be kept consistent in terms of both text and visual elements. Changing your message and visuals constantly does nothing but confuse your audience regarding your brand purpose. Keep it clear and simple. In particular, keep it consistent so that all the elements of your brand can register in the minds of your audience. If you communicate one message and communicate it well, your audience will remember your message. Changing one factor or brand element can be done in a simple form, but even then you must take steps to ensure that the brand message does not change drastically from its core values. As you are probably well aware, words and visual elements support and define the brand to a significant degree. These are the basic elements that move the brand from being an intangible idea into being a concept that is a part of the lives of your target audience—into becoming something that belongs.

Music

It used to be that products might have been associated with a "jingle," a little earworm of a catchy song that was written specifically for the product by someone who presumably sat around all day writing jingles. Music is no longer, by and large, in the life of a brand, a catchy little tune. Often, in modern management of brand culture, music is a vital way of associating a brand with a lifestyle, or a trend, or a group with which the strategy planners want to associate the culture of the brand. But it doesn't have to be that specific of an association. It could be just about communicating a certain feeling—something ineffable that will speak well of the brand and the tastes of the people who produce it. In some respects, then, a choice of the music that surrounds a brand is a statement to an audience about the quality of people, in terms of their thoughtfulness, or coolness, or deepness, or emotionalism, as the case may differ from brand to brand

It speaks to the power of finding the right sort of music for a given purpose that in Hollywood there has sprung up a profession that consists of people, generally young people, whose job it is to pore through hard-to-get, obscure, and often independent sources of music to seek out new, different, original music that will be suitable to go with a certain scene or a certain character in a movie.

It goes without saying that music is a powerful way of activating an audience's senses—of going straight into the part of the brain that is in charge of likes and dislikes and also in charge of belonging. As everyone knows, musical choices are powerful ways of defining cultural associations, such as of generation, or political leanings, or stances on social issues, and so forth. Music can suggest such vague qualities as "progressive" or "sedate" or "melancholy"—or music with lyrics can suggest specific things about a product or brand, as Nike famously did by spending big money for the right to use the Beatles' song "Revolution" in one of their advertisements, or as Volkswagen did with a Nick Drake song. As you think about how to communicate your brand, you will do well to keep your ears open. If you aren't a member of the group you're hoping to reach, but your daughter with a full iPod is, you will do well to listen to what she and her friends say about what music works and what music doesn't in terms of how to create a sense of belonging and good feeling among their group.

Whatever source you may draw it from, you will do well not to underestimate the power of a musical association.

The musical component of your brand doesn't even have to have anything to do with marketing or advertising. You can use music in your company as a way of forging brand identity among employees, as a way of speaking to what your company is like, and what it stands for. The right use of music, or even the fact that you're trying to use music creatively, will speak to the kind of company you're trying to build, what kind of brand identity you're shooting for, and the fact that you value artistic expression.

The Continuity of Brand Belonging

The responsibility of the continuity of the sense of brand belonging lies with the organization's top managers, not bottom management or employees. If top management changes the internal life of the organization, such as the corporate culture or the brand culture, or even if the organization faces high turnover rates, these are factors that can destroy brand continuity. Other factors that disrupt continuity are policy changes within the organization and staff changes from bottom to top. Such negative factors can reflect strongly on the brand continuity externally. These sorts of disruptions have serious consequences in the life of the brand's sense of belonging both internally and externally. Such changes and their impacts are all too common in the Middle East. One of the other factors that impacts brand continuity is cost cutting. Perhaps the genius CFO (chief financial officer) failed to properly assess the financial business plan prior to launching the brand. The brand belonging can continue only if top management is patient enough to realize opportunities for the brand both locally and globally. In addition, management must keep brand elements intact according to the nature of the brand from the day the product launches.

The brand belonging process is not as easy as one might think. From the initial phase of the brand as an idea, all the way to the brand's impact with the audience and from there on, innovation is needed to keep the brand alive. Keeping the interest of the audience intact is also important so that the brand can continue to advance in its quest to belong. Change is great, but only change that supports the initial idea of the brand and supports the brand in the direction of growth should be undertaken. At the same time, any changes must be aligned with the core brand values and not drift away from these. The steps to be taken, from the idea phase to the last element of perception, which is the brand being adopted by the audience, are the steps that will help the brand to live in hearts of the audience and to belong.

For example, Starbucks is a well-focused brand, and everywhere you go, you can find a Starbucks every mile or so, so that the brand belongs to nearly every neighborhood and city. Starbucks not only stayed focused but communicated its positioning, "third place from home," very well. The brand belongs to those who have finished work or are in transit between work and home. Starbucks is a great brand that communicated its coffee culture to the hearts of its audience and reached to every three blocks between the office and home.

Many firms try to change the core value of the brand mid-process, or even at times modify the core product value from the original. How in the world can the brand live in the process of belonging if the brand faces constant changes? It can't! In the event of such capricious changes, the brand confuses its target audience as to its purpose and deliverables. Admittedly, one could simplify things and say change is good in order to create interest.

This is absolutely true! But again, constant change will create a negative reaction within the audience. They will start drifting away from the brand because too many things have changed from what they have become accustomed to and to which they have created an emotional attachment.

Such drastic moves are common because business owners act as their own marketers or are influenced by members of the organization who are clueless about the processes of building a long-lasting brand that can sustain growth and become part of a perfect belonging process.

The Marketing Mix: an Underview

I have identified the importance of brand belonging beginning with the principles of marketing. This is called the marketing mix. Among professionals, the marketing mix has evolved until it has become the Seven Ps: product, price, place, promotion, packaging, positioning, and people. The heart of the Seven Ps (or the marketing mix) is the birth of any great tactical marketing strategy that will ultimately lead to the process of belonging. For an idea to become a product, the idea must be well tested and sound from the point of view of a defined prospective target audience (the people). Here the people is used in a general sense, but in due time, the brand will become more focused in terms of an intended target audience. Once you have focused your brand, then you can build the process of belonging between the product value and consumers' expectations. Remember—this is just one of the seven components that is needed to build the belonging process.

You must have a basic knowledge of your audience and their behavior. What are their likes, what are the pertinent facts of their culture, and how can these be linked to your product, packaging, price, positioning, and place? Each of these elements has a way to become aligned with the product so that one identity can deliver the message that leads to belonging. For example, the price depends on the income bracket and what segment you are targeting to create the belonging process. Each segment of the target audience has its own characteristics with regard to price acceptance. Place is another example. If your brand is an affluent brand, then the place where it belongs is in an upscale location. If your brand is positioned as a luxury item, then the segment is upper-class affluent. As an example, if the package of the brand builds the perception that it is an expensive product from the point of view of the target audience, then the packaging belongs to the upper-class audience. The center of attention in the belonging process is the target audience. Everything should be aligned in order to bring about consistency with regard to how the brand is communicated to that audience so that the brand can be focused to reach that audience and then to belong to them. The same examples apply in reverse for a lower-price product.

When you think of belonging in terms of the Sevens Ps, each P identifies an element by which all the brand's qualities may reach the heart of the audience and come to belong to that audience. Each element or point of the brand must be aligned with the audience—high price/high class; expensive packaging/high-end places; high product quality/communication through high-end advertising mediums. For a brand targeting a lower-end audience, then all Seven Ps change to the opposite orientation. But if all is done well, and with a real sense of relationship with the potential consumers, the product will still come to belong in the heart of the audience.

Emotions

For the brand to become tangible—in the case of a service—then emotion is one of the strongest attributes. The same applies for products that are tangible, but the emotional attachment for a service must be stronger. Emotional connections have several impacts for a brand. They help consumers establish a buying habit and create a lasting impression of the kind of service that supports the brand belonging in the heart of the audience. Using the vehicle of the five senses, you can activate your prospects' emotional reaction to your brand. When emotion is provided through an experience, the impression left can also generate word-of-mouth advertising that can help the public relations platform of the brand. Your audience will feel emotions through their perceptions and through the personal service they receive. These considerations keep the audience intact, and they will help you find a larger audience such that your brand will reach its goal.

For example, have you ever walked into a luxury hotel where, starting from your experience as you step in the door, the concierge gives you your first impression of the hotel? His facial and verbal communication can brighten your day as he guides you to the front desk and assists you with your belongings. This simple experience of two steps is an example of emotional impact. Even if this is only your first impact, the emotions you experience will motivate you to come back to the same brand with the same expectations.

Innovation

What keeps the brand interest active? Your audience will not remain interested in your brand merely based on innovation, but you must constantly update the brand and stay in touch with market changes in order to keep up with trends. Indeed, you must search for trends, particularly leading trends. When a brand leads a trend, it holds a strong point of interest with the audience, and in such a leadership role the brand should be consistent. Innovating the brand means not making total changes, but continually adding value in order to keep the interest moving and to keep the audience exploring the brand. When a brand belongs to an audience, that audience wants to see what's new with the experience and how the brand changes. The brand should still adapt to the audience's lives as it did from the beginning.

I have found that direct activity with the brand in terms of operating from a public relations platform is one strong trendsetter, as long as the brand is active through sponsorship beyond just advertising and customer service. The brand should show its communication commitment to the audience. In the case of today's social media, adaptability can come from continuing to update the brand platform through its diversity of services. These services should engage the audience directly with each of the brand's elements. Many companies have failed to stay in motion with their brands. In the case of one major online social media, however, it has attained world dominance by providing the service in different languages that accommodate diverse needs. Innovation never stops a brand from belonging; instead, it drives the brand farther toward the initial and ultimate goal.

When thinking about innovation, look, for example, at things that were made back in the early 1900s as brands. If they were kept until today the way they were, with only minor changes from generation to generation, the brands would have been long dead in terms of their belonging. A brand should be innovative in all its elements, but it must also consider changes to communication and new platforms on which to appear. Brands are alive. They must adapt to change rather than just rejecting change and life and trying to muddle by the way they are until they find themselves dead. Brands do die a natural death, but the responsibility for their deaths in the Middle East usually lies with the brand owners or the business owners who take the need for change as a negative reflection on them on a personal level rather viewing it as a way of reaching for continuous growth. Innovation is the heart of today's business world, and differentiation is what ensures that a brand stands out so as to thrive.

The Differentiation of Belonging

I have witnessed many brands launched successfully. Among those I have witnessed was a replication or, as we call it in marketing and communication, a "Me2 brand." How in the world can the second look-alike brand belong when the original has already broken through the thick wall surrounding human emotions and reached the audience at its heart? Some might say "just differentiate" the segment or change positioning, and a Me2 brand will succeed. Well, of course, it will survive, but the process of belonging will not have the same long-term impact as it did for the first product in the category. Differentiation is what keeps a brand alive today in cluttered industries. When brands seem to be similar in all respects, the audience will resort to the brand they have experienced previously.

An illustration of this idea comes to mind concerning a typical investor in the Middle East who takes the easy way out, simply replicating what already exists. Later, due to lack of a proper marketing experience, disaster hits when the brand dies. The differentiation factor is not a change in the target audience's habits or the way a brand is supposed to be, but it is a way to create a new category to which a brand can belong so that it can become the dominant brand. Differentiation can proceed from many different areas of branding, not just by building a new category. It also can proceed from finding a way to provide an innovative product or creating a differentiation profile. Differentiation can also come through positioning, a differentiated communication plan, or via several other elements. Differentiation is applied knowing that your brand will enter a tight category and needs to distinctly stand out from its competitors. If the differentiation is about providing an innovative product, then you will be the first to hold the category. Always attempt in whatever you do to create proper differentiation so that you are either the first or the second in the category you enter, not the tenth or eleventh.

Remember the rule of seven: the mind can remember only up to seven items at any time but permanently remembers only the first two items. Further than that, consider that you have on your hands a furious war in the marketplace because you never bothered to apply the differentiation factor to your brand.

The next section involves a case study that illustrates a differentiation factor we all have witnessed in the Middle East. The chance for us to survive in this furious global market is to accept change and dwell with it, work along with it, and not try to resist it. We need our brands to belong in the global market and not merely our neighborhoods. How can this be done if we are witnessing global brands enter our domain, but we build brands that rarely enter the global market platform, or possibly which enter but are rejected because of their being mere replication? I urge you to swallow a little pride, accept change, and listen to marketers who have the expertise, and perhaps the emotional detachment, to help you achieve your goals.

Brand Strategy

Where does your brand strategy start? Do you think your brand strategy belongs only to the communication phase? Is buying time to advertise your product your brand strategy? Well, you are very wrong, my friend, very! You heard me! Following such a strategy, your brand life will be doomed before you know it. Brand strategy is a larger picture of drafting a life for the brand. It evolves just like anything in life—from an idea, to a name, to an identity, to a personality, to its personal character, and to its culture. Whoever neglects these factors is not building a brand but merely building a logo.

An example of the folly of using advertising alone as a strategy in the Middle East is the case of luxury cars. Dealers love to use mass-market communication tools! "It's the billboard! The most expensive! This will show how strong we are!" These are the nuances of the thinking: that is, that certain communications only work well with mass-market auto dealer agents and so on. How many of those cars are on the road? Was it the presence of a communications strategy, or was it that the advertising agency figured that the reach of communication could bring in sales? When I think of luxury cars and mass marketing, another question pops into my mind: aren't tools of communication supposed to be segmented just as target audiences are? Yes! It's the competitive edge! Why, I wonder, and how, since their direct competition hardly ever use those media?

The issue should not be how expensive is the media that is used. Instead, the concern here should be who is the target audience? Will their audience recognize the value based on the media, and will that recognition of value bring the brand to a position of belonging? From my experience, if a brand tries to position itself as a luxury brand, then it should not underrate the appropriateness of media for advertising. Billboards are not for luxury cars unless they appear on a branded street in New York, Paris, Milan, or Jeddah's Tahlia Street. The empowerment of influence comes only if you can identify where the brand should belong, with what it should be associated, and its influence on the tool of communication medium used. Simply take for your model the language of association. Luxury brands belong on luxury platforms. The issue is not how much you pay; instead, it is which medium your intended audience grasps. The downfall of an advertising agency is when it tries to act as a marketer.

The primary factor after the idea and the audience is your brand positioning, which is the primary part of your brand strategy. Then comes the name, which will fit the lives of the audience and engage them. Remember, don't choose just any name, but choose a name that has a chance of belonging to the target audience. This profile process relates to the strategy of branding regarding what colors to use. Depending on what industry, not just any colors will be appropriate. Each industry has specific colors that have evolved with that industry, with which the audience identifies, and through which the audience perceives the brand and understands what it stands for. For example, when is green used? Whenever you have anything that deals with agriculture or biofuel, you will see green. When do you see black? You often see black whenever you have a brand that is positioned as prestigious or otherwise highly elevated. Colors and how you used them do matter. After colors comes the design. Depending on the audience and the targeted segment of the market, design (shape) can simply communicate visually even apart from colors.

When designing a name, even certain fonts belong somewhere. For example, the heavy metal music fonts are identified with sharp edges. The same goes for gothic and food shapes, for example. Fonts are well identified, and millions of brands have worked through them. When thinking of positioning, you must think first of brand differentiation in the midst of any heavily populated category. What would you like your audience to perceive? What do you have in mind? When you decide what you want the consumer to perceive, write your positioning in a few sentences. Then think deeply about those sentences and how they can be translated into a tagline that will resonate with your target audience.

An example in this regard comes from the Saudi market and concerns the local telephone company that sells landline service, the Internet, and cell phones and that operates under one company umbrella called Saudi Telecom. This company has recently relaunched itself with the tagline "Easier life," which was designed by JWT, the global advertising agency. In this move, the company was, through this tagline, now claiming that it operated from a position of its activities revolving around the customers' needs. However, within a short period of time the local audience made a joke out of the tagline because the company failed miserably to exhibit the deliverables. In addition to the service failure, I think the audience found the tagline hard to relate to any of the three services the company offered. The brand held out "Easier life" as the tagline for each service, so that your landline with its technology is for an easier life, your cell phone with Internet service is for an easier life, your Internet at home or the office is for an easier life. The tagline was so extended that the products were soon living in a void. Second, the cell phone brand was called Al Jawal, which is a great name, since all consumers in Saudi call cell phone in Arabic *Al Jawal* (the handset). The Saudi telecom company in its future strategy decided to void the brand name out and keep all three services under one name. Given that the company enjoys a monopoly of landline service, yes they have no competition, but with regard to their cell phone and Internet offerings, their future growth is at risk if they don't brand these out separately, giving each of the services its own brand name.

This is all great, but the one thing the company failed to deliver was the brand promise implied by its brand strategy when it had internal problems in terms of operational function. For this reason, consumer complaints increased, and the new identity with its great positioning seemed to fail. How great is positioning and what it can do for a brand! But, at the same time, if the total brand strategy deliverable is not in place, then expect that the brand will fail. What about brand culture? Why do you need brand culture? Brand culture supports the total heart of brand belonging so that the brand lives. Think about it! Is hip-hop a culture? Yes! It's also a brand exported by the US that generated billions of dollars. Brands do need to have culture in order to attain loyal followers. By gaining brand followers you are creating a movement that controls change while you sustain the basic principles by which the brand was born.

The brand environment is the actual experience that the consumer undergoes. It is intended to be part of your brand strategy. Yes, my friend, brands do belong to their audience, just like we belong to our parents. Brands have a beginning and an end, a birth and a death. They may have a natural death or suffer a death by mismanagement. So make sure you understand the basic principles of your brand strategy prior to engaging in enormous spending. The brand environment is also the experience the target audience undergoes in order to feel the brand in a more tangible way. This process occurs primarily in the service industry and can leave a lasting impression. Think of airlines, hotels, and retail outlets, for example. The brand environment is crucial when building a strategy for a service. It carries the brand further and assures the brand has the chance to exist longer. The importance of the brand environment, as we who are involved in business in these parts know, is taken all too lightly in our region of the Middle East. We live in our own world of assumptions, and we decide what is good for the consumer rather than having the consumer be the CEO of our firm.

Chapter 11:

A CALL TO ACTION

The Need for a Marketing Association in the Middle East

One of my ongoing concerns is whether I will ever see a day when the art of marketing, with all its nuances, is implemented to full effect in our region. Will I ever see any of our homegrown FMCGs flourish on a global scale rather than just in the local markets? For instance, why wasn't it an Arab company that adopted the great visual icon and the well-known name of the Bedouin as a brand, instead of letting somebody in Australia who sells tents take the idea? I am a passionate marketing advocate whose goal is to see any one of our consumer brands on supermarket shelves around the globe. This will never happen, however, unless those in the local market accept that they must educate themselves on the basic principles of marketing.

While the concept of brand positioning was articulated by Al Ries and Jack Trout some twenty years ago, it has only reached our region comparatively recently. Many marketers and ad agencies have yet to adopt the full principles of positioning. This lag demonstrates just how far behind we are in terms of adapting and transforming. This lag is dangerous when we consider how far off we are, especially in this era of globalization, when many brands are synchronized perfectly within one point or place through innovations such as e-commerce. Will the next generation of young marketers face these changes proactively and recognize the potential financial rewards that follow? What follows is my call to action.

First, we must establish a regional marketing association that will help brand owners fulfill their potential. This association would refer brand owners to professionals who can assist with brand building and find models that will benefit owners within a larger spectrum.

We must start from a home base in all industries and initiate an oversight panel. Let's work together to enable our market to flourish! I am asking for everyone's involvement—from all countries in our region—to set up this association. It will help us penetrate all possibilities for our brands.

We are a well-equipped society with enormous potential, and deploying an association might be hard at first. There is always a starting point, however, and perhaps that start will come from this book. We have the manpower, the financials, and the institutions to succeed. We are much more affluent than many regions, but we are so far missing the necessary initiative and guidelines.

Second, I earnestly ask that we redefine the meaning of "marketing" in Arabic and move away from the word "*Tasweeq*." The ambiguity of this word does not help its effectiveness. *Tasweeq* merely implies shopping, sales, and getting products off the shelves. Redefining the meaning is a first step in the right direction.

Third, we should add marketing as a major in the university syllabus as an alternative to general business administration majors.

Fourth, we should encourage community involvement and create public awareness of marketing's principles, its purposes, and its value.

Fifth, and finally, it will take every firm, every marketer, and every organization to move forward as a team. One day we, the Arabs, will have our brands visible in the lives of all global consumers and be on a par with competitive foreign multinationals.

If we can pull together and manage this, we will see growth and change in how we think of marketing and of what it is. Bringing our companies up to date in terms of basic marketing principles is a crucial step for our organizations and for the livelihood of our people.

A Final Note

When I thought of writing this book, I thought of how our region suffers from improper brand building and even a lack of knowledge of the basic principles of marketing. We are way behind in setting our footprint on the global wall, because we have neglected the importance of marketing and decided to go with the power of our own individual minds as some sort of miracle that creates and provides solutions. This book about belonging prescribes solutions comprised of processes, all of which are designed to show how belonging is vitally important in order for brands to live in the life of the audience. Great marketers have written books about many aspects of marketing, including such "greats" as Philip Kotler, Al Ries, and Jack Trout. We must learn from those who are miles ahead of us. We don't want to just replicate what they have created, but we at least want to start where they left off in order to create and nourish our own ideas to meet the needs of the target audience we want to reach.

I have been very active in espousing the importance of marketing for several years. So far, however, I have gained little support locally in my efforts to enhance the process of marketing. One day, based on this book and perhaps others that our own regional marketers write, the region will embrace the principles that we all expect are needed for our products to turn around and work. Establishing an organization within the region such as a marketing association is crucially important in order to provide oversight and guidance in ensuring that marketing models are working as designed and to serve as a resource for those who seek marketing insight.

Chapter 12:

THREE CASE STUDIES— AN "OUTRODUCTION"

This book could have begun with a story of what prompted me to write it, that is, with what follows below as the book's introduction. But I wanted to begin my book with a vision of the future and not of the past. Nevertheless, there is a story behind this book, and it comes out of a past fraught with difficulty and frustration. While I wanted to start this book with ways we can do it right, instead of ways we've done it wrong, I still think it's important to talk about what has gone wrong. It's my hope that by sharing those difficulties and frustrations here at the end of the book, in my "outroduction," that I can not only provide the vision that precedes this section with some context, but that I can give wings to the project of changing the way marketing is done by showing you a slice of the alternative.

Case Study: What Is "Marketing," Exactly?

Branding something in order to sell it is what branding does. A brand is more than a logo, a slogan, or a design. Branding uses an extraordinary combination of elements to calibrate and align the product to the target audience and build name recognition. Brand builders must consider the multi-leveled process involved in branding, which encompasses various steps to create a living brand—from the moment the idea is conceived to the daily experience the brand has with the target consumer.

The importance of brand building in today's economy is key to boosting not only a brand's perception but the culture around it. The focal measure of the brand's communication is the idea, the value, and the personality of that brand. Everything about the brand must be aligned effectively, including its overall personality, so that the consumer understands, appreciates, and desires the product.

Reverse Flow

The initial stage of building an idea and transforming it into a brand is identifying the need and the presumed contribution the brand brings to its users. This process assists in establishing a totally involved—indeed, an emotional—connection with the brand. Brand building then takes a product from brand "X" through the full circle of creation into becoming a "living" thing.

The flawed belief that branding is merely an "art form" that revolves around colors and logos is an overriding misimpression that becomes the culprit that causes some firms in the Middle East to lose face. This ill-informed belief leads to enormous failures in market penetration, as well as a great deal of lost opportunity. The main contributor to this misunderstanding is that today anyone can obtain a license to open an advertising agency, which will then offer only such trappings as logo design and print services.

Local and multinational advertising agencies in the Middle East are facing a backlash from inexperienced competitors who present misconceptions to their clients. The true circle of branding is viable only when an idea is constructed intensely and is carefully thought out by both the business owner and his marketing department. This circular flow continues with the advertising agency or design studio charged with building the personality of the idea into a brand ID. The agency develops the visual elements of the brand by implementing the conceptual visions and ideas of the company that is developing the product. A marketing consultant with expertise in the brand-building process is needed to ensure the strategy flows and to build the required models. In this way, the advertising agency will have a better vision of its deliverables.

Around in Cycles

Today we can observe many brands on the supermarket shelves declining in sales. This occurs because the average marketing department in local manufacturing believes that total product equity is the primary ingredient to success rather than the needs of the target audience. They hold tightly to this misconception both in terms of the product profile and how they communicate their brand. This situation has caused the Middle East market to face an enormous clutter of FMCGs that are locally produced or imported.

The competitive advantage between regional products and imports has always centered on the pricing strategy. Regional manufacturers prefer to be more price-competitive in their attempts to dominate a market segment; usually, however, price strategy alone without differentiating factors results in brand failure. The imported product always assumes a higher-end target audience in terms of price, packaging, and communication. Imported product marketers also formulate better marketing and tactical strategies to create a connection between their brands and their target audiences.

The difference between regional production and imports, however, is not the main issue; instead, the issue is the total brand value positioning. Regional producers underestimate the value of marketing strategy, proper communication, and the total life cycle of a brand.

Some of the regional firms fail to innovate a brand within its life cycle, so that ultimately, that brand faces a generational decline. Take for example the sectors of confectionery and beverages that are produced regionally. These brands have existed for the past thirty years. Once they dominated their markets. However, they have failed to keep up with new generational needs and trends. Instead, their total market share has declined drastically as key international players entered the void this failure left in the market.

Degeneration Next

One of the basic reasons for this "degeneration" is that these brands kept their first generation of consumers happy, but completely failed to attract a second generation. Essentially, they slept while market competition emerged through the years. Brands have to keep innovating to deal with changes in the cultural environment and new buying trends.

Here is where I see that many of the Middle East's regionally produced brands are failing to establish the proper continuity of their brand life cycle.

Secondary misconceptions can also result from a marketing department that relies on an advertising agency to provide results in terms of potential brand penetration. Instead, the marketing department should firmly hold the key responsibility of identifying the many elements of a brand strategy prior to an advertising agency producing any communications.

Confusion about what marketing does versus what advertising does creates havoc in creating a brand—both in terms of due diligence and of the set-up process. Moreover, it muddles the actual working processes of the marketing departments of local firms. Some often confuse the word "marketing" with "sales," while others think that "advertising" is actually marketing.

These factors regarding misconceptions in branding create confusion about brand penetration or non-brand penetration. These factors also consequently produce enormous waste in the resources of the actual marketing department—and they jeopardize the process of brand building and belonging.

Today, having a proper brand that fulfills a need, dominates a category, and is well focused toward its target audience can bring the sort of end results the business owner wants.

Case Study: Differentiation

A success story for one brand does not apply to all brands. The reality of life is that once a consumer has a successful experience with a particular brand, an incoming new brand must differentiate itself in order to compete. It must do so either by market segmentation or by creating a total brand proposition for the target audience.

There are, indeed, spaces for the newly created category, but only a few. If differentiation does not come with the new brand, you can consider it dead.

The reality of the Middle Eastern market is a lack of innovation or creativity. We move quickly to copy one success story; in a few months to a year you will find six to seven brands trying to copy the success story of the first brand. The funny thing is that most of the newcomers' board members sit around and focus their efforts on market share. Is their market share growing? Are they spending enough on advertising to increase market share by 5 percent? How much money will the company need to dump into advertising to gain market share? If we spend millions, how will we earn a return? Unfortunately, these are not the right questions.

We must be very realistic here. At times, in some companies, the marketing department is good for nothing. That's because their understanding of marketing is basically limited to advertising; in other words, appearing on every medium possible, whether or not that medium truly targets their core audience. They go simply for what they call "presence." Think of a brand such as Starbucks. It's a mega-brand known worldwide, but do you see ads for it everywhere? Hardly! Yet, you see Starbucks stores everywhere. In major cities, you can probably see the stores on every street corner.

I hope this book has the power to change minds about marketing in the Middle East. It's all about *market planning*. What strategies do you need to implement to address your target audience and fulfill their needs? The sad reality of our region is that we move fast when we see that something is working for someone else. We decide to launch our own version and fight tooth and nail. The ironic beauty of it is that we hammer the consumer with the word "quality." Consumers' confidence in our brands has dropped tremendously because the reality of our deliverables does not align with what the brands promise.

We take the world of marketing and creativity very lightly. We consider a brand as if it were just a logo printed on a printing press. Well, gentlemen, if you are reading this book, you must admit that you have just realized that the overall marketing process in today's world is a lot different from what it was during the days of your forefathers' trade. Copying other models that work does not assist us in breaking into the market. It demonstrates a complete lack of innovation and a failure to build up an idea using proper marketing models.

Once—and I have witnesses for this—an investor asked me to replicate something that he had seen working in the local market. It was the dominant brand in the market, and there was no way I was willing to put my neck on the line. The brand was the first in the category and was known for its strong selling propositions. The brand was well registered with its target audience—enough so that when you mentioned the brand name, it was easy for the average consumer to tell you what the product line was. I sat in my house and thought about my conversation with this investor. What was he thinking? Why couldn't he try to become dominant in another area, instead of trying to break into a market where he knew that he had no chance?

Here comes the point of risk. Most investors are risk-takers, but you have to have proper insight into the market to take even a minimal risk. In our region a "good" risk is calculated as one that copies another. That is the most risk you will encounter, and it is not even minimal. Our region is exceptionally risk-averse with regard to new ideas. Many people in business will not try to create a new category; they'd rather work with what exists. This is why we are limited to so few industries. If you sell a car, that's a great business. A few years later, you will see a million car dealers and agents popping up around the Middle East to try to sell their cars. The same applies to other products in our region.

Case Study: Middle East Errors in Marketing

I have just returned from a meeting in which I watched the business owner working on the concept of his new project and its brand personality. To my disbelief, he was totally disregarding the behavior and needs of his intended target audience. Yet, in branding, these considerations are a core concept. When I asked the owner on what basis he was building the concept, he answered, "Market research." Period.

I wondered if he knew how general a category "market research" is. And, further, does he know or wonder how you can hire a multinational communications firm to work on your brand without having even a clear marketing plan and strategy? The gap between market research and marketing strategy is huge! Who will fill the gap? The owner? I don't think so.

My argument is that our products and services will bleed and perish without the insight provided by marketing principles. When will business owners understand this? As a man who is half Saudi, my anger ignites when I see a business owner "working" on his products or services regardless of whether what he's doing makes sense or not. The owner's answer, inevitably, is "it has to be done" or that the choice is his. Working from this attitude, the brand will hit rock bottom because the businesses owner never acknowledges his initial errors in the process. Then, when the product fails, the owner fires every department manager and blames them for lost investments. This whole cycle could be avoided with careful attention to marketing strategy.

These owners must also realize that the finance and marketing departments need to be inextricably connected. Some owners, whether qualified or not, appoint themselves as the company's financial manager. They totally disregard the process of establishing a proper financial department and then linking it to the marketing department. These owners then face the marketing department and ask if they can increase the company's profits. Without either department properly set, are they supposed to produce miracles? Further, owners rely too much on advertising agencies to provide them a "complete" branding strategy, while agencies would love to deliver a job without marketing insight in order to make their buck. Ought we to hold the ad agency responsible for the entire brand? No! The agency's job is to deliver the brand communication—only one piece of the puzzle. But, in the mind of the owner, that ad agency should attain all sales results.

The dilemma here is twofold: first, the owner of the brand decides the fate of the brand from its inception. But how? And why? Second, when will business owners work as a team with all the departments within their organizations, delegating efforts to the experts? Business owners should avoid the "one-man show" attitude that inevitably keeps the brand and the organization stagnant. In those scenarios, the business owner works on the product, the business owner decides the colors of the brand ID and designs, the business owner decides to call the advertising agencies to bid for the project, the business owner selects the lowest offer available, the business owner passes the whole entire project to the marketing department. The business owner does the sales forecast; the business owner writes the annual sales goal in a memo to the head of marketing. The business owner decides to fire the marketing department six months from launch … what else did the business owner overlook? Oh, yes. Then he decided to hire his son, a fresh graduate, to the post of head of marketing.

The problem here is that the fundamental principles of marketing are not in place, or at best, the marketing mix has been given only cursory thought. My prediction in this situation is that within six months, the owner will seek help to modify a plan that did not work. Change at this point will be difficult. What has registered as a bad experience with the consumer will be hard to change.

The owner should have considered all this in the initial phases of the project. How you brand a product and implement a marketing strategy should always be based on your target audience. How you build the profile of the brand and how you communicate the brand's mission should be based on the target audience. Creating a brand is like building a marriage between the brand and the audience. If you don't manage the brand, then the union will dissolve and turn to hatred, and the brand will decline.

Further, branding is not only important to your external audience, but also to your internal audience—how do your employees perceive your brand? Is it the same way you would expect your consumer audience to perceive your brand? If you can think of the brand as replicating human nature from inception to growth, you will be successful. The way you manage your child's life—investing time and tools in him that empower him to succeed—is also how you should manage your brand.

The realization that change must happen in our region will hit business owners hard when they understand the facts completely. Our collective responsibility should be to our region. To date, individual efforts have not focused on global branding because business owners have only a short-term vision. They must understand the issues and change their vision to one that looks to the long term.

The funniest thing happened. I witnessed a company owner telling his employees that he had been restructuring for the past seven months. In the course of that discussion he explained how he had disregarded every process that was working. This moment arose because he had surrounded himself with people that were clueless about what modern business structures are. As a consultant, I asked myself, how in the world can I assist such a company when the owner himself is clueless about marketing and the most basic principles of marketing have no place in his thinking? How in the world will marketing ever properly flourish when the owners of the businesses—who are originally trade merchants, by and large—look at marketing as mere pocket change? It's a complete joke how the owners can be so hardheaded and believe that they know it all!

Who was to blame, however, when I am called to assist in lifting the brand back up after the owner has decided to sideline the marketing director? During the report and in dissecting the brand's life, I observed that the brand had enjoyed a great reaction and was moving in the right direction. In my view, the marketing director had done a great job. Because both parties didn't see eye to eye, however, the owner decided to sideline him to restructure the company. Unfortunately, the brand declined in the market.

In thinking about fixing this problem, I realized that the target audience had gone through a horrible experience with the brand, and to change their minds would be one heck of a "mission impossible" at this point. I will never understand how and why a business owner who has never had experience in raising brands, could take the critical actions he did. Was it an ego issue based on "I'm right and you're wrong"? If not, what was it exactly? The cost of repair is quite expensive, and this scenario was the exact result of a company being placed in that situation. I declared this even to the point of actually saying that most business owners in our region are trade merchants rather than businessmen.

A die-hard incident such as this is shocking for me, especially when the owner of the business has no clue what marketing is or how to apply its principles, or even about the scientific thinking underlying marketing. It is my belief that such owners should not be brand owners and should merely focus on trading as merchants. Owners are not aware that brands are like humans: that they grow gradually and then the owner should step aside and let "those who know" implement the complete plan for moving the brand forward. It pains me that many brands I have seen have enormous potential to excel, but due to the lack of the owner's understanding about marketing, the results have been catastrophic.

Such incidents are quite common in our region, and it is very hard to convince owners, especially those whose minds seem inextricably set in their ways. I have learned one thing, and that is to never, ever correct an owner or you will be blamed for their plight. But, if you do as they please, you will still be blamed for the failure of the brands.

My key advice to the next director of marketing who is sidelined is to find out first what the business owner's insights are into marketing. If you find the same story as the one you have experienced, move on even if the pay is tempting. Let the business owners live what I have experienced. I have learned not to count on the possibility of change, because such change will never take place among those who do not wish to change their business practices.

I personally declined the account noted above because I was not convinced that the owner had enough business ability to make a real plan work, and I believed that his vision was skewed. His mind was set that his brand must attain enormous cash results quickly. But how? Some business owners suppose that their newly minted brand should produce an extraordinary revenue within six months to a year. Others expect that will happen in three years, based on the basic principles of marketing. How about those who use the full array of processes of scientific strategy thinking, brand processes, and market expansion plans based on opportunity? For example, did Michael Dell expect that Dell would be a mega-brand? What was his initial strategy? Did Facebook derive its current strategy from its starting strategy? Let's talk it out! If brands are like humans, they must grow gradually and must be well fed and pampered. In this case, the owner did not wish to feed and pamper the brand, but instead to drain it to the last drop. Such scenarios are endless in our region. Until the new generation Y comes in, all I can say is, may God bless our homegrown brands.

As marketers, we all hope that business owners will hear our message and understand the importance of marketing in any given business. If marketing is taken lightly and disregarded, then no change will take place. To me, the importance of marketing and an awareness of its importance are a must. Such awareness must be spread to all business owners in order to create a change in thinking about what modern marketing applications really are.

Chapter 13:

CLOSING THOUGHTS: WHY WE SHOULD CARE

So, this is my vision of the solutions, and this is my vision of the problems. I truly appreciate your spending this time with me, allowing me to share my experiences and my deep passion for marketing and for sharing with me so much of your valuable time and attention. As I close, I'd like to take one further step back, beyond sharing how marketing can be good for business, to how I think good marketing and the good business it produces are important for all of us. I try to keep in mind as I work and write what the point of all this is. With that in mind, reminding myself of what the point is, herewith are a few thoughts about why all this is important to me—about why we should care whether people use good marketing practices or not, and indeed why we should care whether businesses do well or not. Why not do things as we've always done, or as we feel like doing, and let the chips fall where they may? Why so much intensity concerning how to improve?

My first answer to those questions is simple: the best reason to do business better isn't to make more money, or to move us all into the twenty-first century, or for us all to become more efficient, although all those things are admirable goals. The first reason to do business better is simple. It's because when it comes to the prospects of a given business, it's not just money, but people's livelihoods, well-being, and happiness that are at stake.

It's easy, when contemplating things as lofty as strategies and forecasts, or indeed things as intricate and as detailed as colors and fonts, to lose sight of the fact that a bad decision in terms of brand positioning, for instance, or in failing to differentiate a product, doesn't just mean a product might fail. It may also mean a business fails. In that case, I often need to remind myself that it's not just some abstract entity that's folding, something we can shrug or even laugh off when we see the little blurb about it in the business section of the newspaper.

It's also, in the first place, the primary stakeholders, such as owners, board members, shareholders and so on, who stand to lose. I don't need to tell you that ill fortune that befalls even people who are well-insulated from calamity in terms of their income class can have widespread effects on an economy. When bad fortune befalls the stock market based on bad business performance, it effectively means that everyone in the country, and even worldwide, is a stakeholder in what happens in that business.

In the second place, it's the employees of a failed business who will bear the brunt of the consequences of a failed product. They have fewer resources than owners and other stakeholders by which to absorb such a blow. Employees, like businesses, are easy to think about in the abstract and the plural, such that people may lose sight of the specific man or woman who has children to feed, neighbors' gossip to worry about, and bills to pay; it is easy to forget that all the suffering that comes with economic hardship is very real.

And the suffering that comes with economic hardship doesn't just stop with a lack of money, or a downturn, and it doesn't just stop with employees. The money they don't make doesn't get spent, and pretty soon the effect ripples out. Economic hard times can make an entire people angry and frustrated. When we're angry and frustrated, we tend not to make the best decisions, and things can get even worse.

Thus, this pursuit is important because business failure has a direct correspondence with human suffering.

The second reason to care has to do with what business is, apart from a way to make money. Freud said that what a person needs to be happy is love and work. Work isn't just a way to make money. For many of us, our work is a fundamental part of the definition of who we are. When people ask you who you are, if they have occasion to do so, wouldn't one of your first answers be to name your profession?

This acknowledgment of the link between one's work and one's identity, and conversely then, between who we are as people and how that translates into what we do at work, leads me to my last point. For me, doing marketing better isn't just about paving the way to better profits, or even about staving off economic hardship. Given that our profession is an integral part of who we are, I believe that doing our work better has the potential of making each of us a better person and of making us, whoever we are, a better people.

One of the things I'm most encouraged about is a growing awareness among the smartest and best-informed people who do business that doing things right, not merely in the sense of following accepted practices, but doing things right in the sense of honoring the best principles of our most sacred and time-honored teachings, is also turning out to be the scientifically demonstrated best way to create a sustainable, profitable business.

You may have noticed that there is something very like a set of basic, time-honored values underlying much of what modern marketing is about, as we've discussed it in this book. These values include consideration, for instance, both of potential customers and their needs and desires and of employees and their need to feel valued, respected, and listened to and to have extended to them the very basic sort of justice—not to mention common courtesy—that means that their hard work will be fairly rewarded. Communication, too, is another value in play here, in which regard we're not just talking about getting out the word about the brand, but making sure our deeds match our claims. Doing that one, simple thing—doing as we say we will do, practicing what we preach—puts us in line with one of the oldest and best definitions of what it means to live out the values of honor and integrity.

I take it as simultaneously a vindication of our time-honored values and of our best, most modern business practices that each tends to validate the other. As a person whose business is business, I feel that I should point out that in today's business world, values are a value.

But the incorporation of these values into what we do isn't just for our sake in the quest for self-improvement. It's also, to a certain extent, about self-preservation, in a business sense. There's a trend that's been ongoing in the United States for quite some time and is making inroads here (and in this case I see that movement as a good thing) in which people, in making buying decisions, have begun to evaluate not merely the product, but the character and conduct of the entity that is selling it. That is to say, the buying public has begun to ask for social responsibility, or just plain good values, on the part of its vendors.

Examples of the power of this movement are three juggernauts of business, all brilliant in terms of their marketing and strategy, but all of which were seriously impacted by their failures to maintain a relationship with their audiences, not in terms of their products, but in terms of what the audience expected of them with regard to their being good fellow citizens.

In the first instance, McDonald's, which for years was unassailable as a business force and was held out as a paragon of how businesses ought to do business, suddenly, beginning in the '90s, found itself not only struggling to keep up with its legendary quality control and service expectations, but struggling to ameliorate the fact of its brand increasingly being associated with waste, depletion, exploitation, and unhealthy lifestyle choices. McDonald's, among many other large companies, was forced to look to the ways it did business in order to maintain its flagging customer base.

In the case of McDonald's, the company found that it needed to stay in touch with its audience, not just in terms of what products they wanted to consume, and not just how those products were made, but also in terms of whether McDonald's was the sort of company that was doing good, by and large, or whether it was operating just for profit. As a result, McDonald's not only cleaned up its act on several fronts; it also became a major player in terms of charitable giving.

Another major example of a faltering juggernaut was the case of Wal-Mart, which, fairly or not, had to position itself as a leader in terms of environmental responsibility in order to turn around a brand perception that the company was on the bad side of the ledger in terms of environmental matters.

But it is the banking industry in America that is the signal example of the need for following best business practices. In the case of that industry, their failure wasn't one of mere public perception, failing to keep up with various trends to save rainforests or dolphins or to go solar. In the case of that industry, the failure was a very concrete matter based at the heart of what they supposedly did best—dealing with their products and services. And of course the failure didn't impact just a business, or the families associated with that business; it affected the entire globe. As it was, it was a disaster; it could have been a catastrophe.

What that collapse of some of the strongest, most respected concerns on the entire globe demonstrated to those of us who are in business—or what it should have demonstrated if we had been paying attention—is that there is no such thing as a person in business who is so rich and powerful as to be insulated from the most dismal dishonor and failure. That there is no one so smart and savvy in such a high-tech-bolstered industry that he or she can't mess things up royally, and almost permanently. That the best of us can make terrible mistakes based on shortsightedness and greed. That there is no one who's so good and honored that they get a pass to fly above the rules the rest of us live by.

Finally, the experience of the banking industry in America demonstrates that the smartest, most respected, and best-informed among us can be wrong, and that we would all do well to continually bring to bear our best information, and our best practices, and our best humility, in the attempt to try to be right, and that the only shame in making changes is in making them too late, or in never making them at all.

So there it is. That's why I think what we do is important. It matters. I hope I've communicated some of my passion for our prospects. I also hope that I've communicated, along with a clear-sighted view of our problems, my great hopes and dreams for my region, and my belief in it, as well as in my people. I'm excited about the prospects of improving marketing practices, not just because I love and am passionate about the field of marketing (and I do, and I am!) but also because I think we and our children, and their children after them, will be a good deal happier and better off if we do.